FRITZ

THE JACKIE ROBINSON OF HIS DAY

AN OUTSTANDING COLLEGIAN
ON THE GRIDIRON
A REMARKABLE PLAYER IN THE NFL
A SUCCESSFUL COACH IN THE NFL

ROBERT LIVINGSTON

BOOKS BY ROBERT K. LIVINGSTON

THE SAILOR AND THE TEACHER

TRAVELS WITH ERNIE

LEAPING INTO THE SKY

BLUE JACKETS

FLEET

HARLEM ON THE WESTERN FRONT

W.T. STEAD AND THE CONSPIRACY OF 1910 TO SAVE THE WORLD

IN THE WAKE OF THE EMPRESS OF CHINA

THE FORGOTTEN CHAPLAIN

AXIS SALLY

THE TARNISHED ROSE

AMERICAN STORIES 1940 - 1960

THE ANCHOR AND THE JOURNALIST

TASTE THE WIND

A DEAN'S LIFE

THEY SAID NO TO WAR

THE OLD GUY IN THE CLASSROOM

FRITZ

NEGRO WEEK AT THE NEW YORK WORLD'S FAIR

DEDICATION

In the spirit of all teachers who seek to understand the past
and struggle to achieve social and economic justice
I dedicate this book.

FRITZ

BOOKS BY ROBERT LIVINGSTON
DEDICATION
TABLE OF CONTENTS

THE POST-GAME SHOW

LEGACIES

HEADLINES

1954 – FRITZ POLLARD WAS INDUCTED INTO THE COLLEGIATE HALL OF FAME

1967 – FRITZ POLLARD ELECTED TO THE RHODE ISLAND HERITAGE HALL OF FAME

1971 – FRITZ POLLARD ELECTED TO THE BROWN UNIVERSITY ATHLETIC HALL OF FAME

1973 – FRITZ POLLARD ELECTED TO THE NATIONAL BLACK HALL OF FAME

1978 – FRITZ POLLARD RECEIVED THE WHITNEY M. YOUNG, JR. MEMORIAL AWARD

1981 – FRITZ POLLARD RECEIVED AN HONORARY DOCTOR OF LETTERS BY BROWN UNIVERSITY

2003 – FRITZ POLLARD SELECTED FOR BROWN'S 125TH ANNIVERSARY ALL-TIME FOOTBALL TEAM

2003 – FRITZ POLLARD ALLIANCE WAS ESTABLISHED TO CHAMPION DIVERSITY IN THE NFL

2005 – FRITZ POLLARD WAS POSTHUMOUSLY INDUCTED INTO THE NATIONAL FOOTBALL HALL OF FAME IN CANTON, OH

2015 – FRITZ POLLARD WAS POSTHUMOUSLY IN-DUCTED INTO THE ROSE BOWL HALL OF FAME IN PASADENA, CA

2019 – FRITZ POLLARD WAS POSTHUMOUSLY IN-DUCTED INTO THE LINCOLN UNIVERSITY HALL OF FAME LOCATED IN OXFORD, PA

2022 – LANE HIGH SCHOOL RENAMED THE FOOT-BALL FIELD IN HONOR OF FRITZ POLLARD

EPILOGUE

Each day the headlines speak to us through the daily newspaper, or by the local radio and television stations, if not by the world of digital communication animating our cell phones, laptops, or the sturdy Apple computer on our desks. This is especially true when dealing with sports coverage. Most of the time we can relate to the blaring headlines. We recognize a name, a place, or an event. We might be a little hazy as to when something happened, but less so as to what actually took place. Occasionally, however, a headline challenges us. We are baffled. We don't have a clue as to the import of the bold print clamoring for our attention. Nor does the penetrating radio voice register with us. Television pictures and film might strike the vaguest memory cord leading to an inner voice crying out, "I've seen that guy, but where?"

Such has been the situation concerning one football player, an elusive running back from Brown University by the name of Fritz Pollard. Hardly anyone recognizes either his name or his accomplishments except for those intimate with football's formative years. Certainly the most rabid fans don't know why he received belated honors. Unfortunately that is often the case with Black-Americans whose talents and achievements were shunted aside by the prevailing white media. However, very much like seeking a vein of gold in the jagged terrain of the Sierra Nevada Mountains one must dig deeply to find the richness below the surface. In the case of Fritz Pollard it is worth the effort.

In uncovering Fritz Pollard's story questions emerge: why did it take so long to recognize this athlete who was the first Black athlete to play in the Rose Bowl in 1916, or who was the second Black football player to gain All-American honors by the noted sports writer, Walter Camp, who called Pollard "one of the greatest runners these eyes have ever seen?" Again, why has the second Black football player inducted into the College Hall of Fame been all but forgotten? Why has the first Black player in professional football been relegated to an almost unknown footnote? Why has the first Black head coach of a professional football team been all but lost to the whims of history? Why do we know so little about the first Black owner of a professional football team, the Brown Bombers? Why has it taken so long for Fritz Pollard's gridiron exploits as a player and coach to be recognized?

There are a few possible reasons. First, what Fritz Pollard did occurred long ago in the early days of both college and professional football, and certainly long before the television and Internet exposure that present day athletes receive. Second, news coverage about sports in his playing days was mainly by local newspapers and later for a few seconds in a radio-news broadcast. National news coverage was on the distant horizon. For much of the country he played in anonymity. Third, the major football accomplishments in Fritz Pollard's life occurred east of the Mississippi and within the Ivy League schools of his day, Harvard, Yale, and Brown universities. There was little notoriety beyond the eastern seaboard. As to professional football coverage it was pretty much limited to the Midwest.

Racial prejudice, of course, cannot be excluded as an explanation for the belated recognition. It wasn't that his exploits on the gridiron were covered up or ignored in a concerted effort to limit the news of a successful Black football player and owner. Nor was there an effort to disparage his skills as a player and coach. That was never an issue. The man could play. He could coach. He had managerial skills as an owner. Those who covered his life in the Black press understood that and provided testimony to his considerable achievements.

Perhaps the simplest answer to explain his lack of name recognition, if not the most unsatisfactory one, is that Fritz Pollard, a Black man, played in a white man's game long ago. He played at a time when the white press provided limited coverage of his prowess on the football field. That was the reality.

Still, the game offered him financial opportunities and a venue to showcase his considerable athletic skills. It also demanded of him a willingness to accede to what we know today as systemic racism. He had to develop survival skills that would permit him to be successful both on and off the football field. In short, he had to tame his natural aggressiveness. He had to find an uneasy path in a world where racial prejudice existed. That said, in the passage of time his story, except for those who really knew about him, simply drifted out of our national consciousness, but not forever.

FRITZ POLLARD

THE PRE-GAME SHOW

"Ability is what you're capable of doing. Motivation determines what you do. At-titude determines how well you do it."

Lou Holtz, Football Coach

CHAPTER 1 – HEADING WEST BY TRAIN

December 22, 1915

The shrill cry of the ponderous locomotive smoke stack blared into the chilly morning air, even as the giant metal wheels sought purchase with the iron rails that would carry the train's great weight. In addition to the usual boxcars and fright carriers there were a number of passenger and Pullman sleeping cars. One of these overnight Pullman cars, really a hotel on wheels, had an unusual passenger list: 26 men, 21 of whom were football players from Brown University. The other five were coaches and aides, and representatives of the school. They were all headed west, first to the Chicago area, a clean shot from Rhode Island, and then by another train these athletic young men would angle south by southwest to New Mexico. Assuming that all went well they would join up with the Southern Pacific Railroad and head for California with high hopes of reaching Pasadena by December 27, 1915. In Chicago the players would have a needed practice at Northwestern University. An additional practice was scheduled at the University of New Mexico in Albuquerque. These temporary stops were necessary to prepare the players for their next game, which would take place in the coming year on January 1, 1916.

The players and others were escorted to the Provident Union Railroad Station by hundreds of Brown students who wanted to give the team a rousing farewell. Whether the students cut class or were excused from classes is still a matter of conjecture. Apparently, many students snake danced to the depot, accompanied by loud cheers and the singing of school fight songs. This was most appropriate. To the everlasting joy of the quiet, if not quaint little campus, the students were waving goodbye to a surprise selection for the 1916 Rose Bowl Game against Washington State College, another unusual choice. Both teams, however, were about to make history in two ways. First, this would be the first Rose Bowl since the 1902 game. After a hiatus of 13 years the New Year's game would be played again in Southern California. Second, the first Black to play in the Rose Bowl and the only Black on the Brown team was on the train. His name was Fritz Pollard.

We are ever true to Brown,
For we love our college dear,
And wherever we may go,
We are ready with a cheer,
And the people always say,
That you can't outshine Brown Bears,
With their Rah! Rah! Rah! and their Ki! Yi! Yi!
And their B-R-O-W-N.

The trip across the country took five days and nights. Commercial air flights were not yet available for the 3,000-mile trip. Nor were cars and buses up for such a trip. America's

15

primitive road system between cities was not yet up to today's standards. By default the "iron horse" would chug the team into history. With little exception few Brown players had ever ventured west of the Mississippi. California for most was the "Wild West," a distant enclave of orange groves, movie studios, and transplanted fellow citizens. Not undone by all this Brown University administrators took out extra insurance on the team, even as the players requested a large container of good old Rhode Island water, sufficient to last them until they reached the "Golden State." That aside every player looked forward to the game and a great adventure.

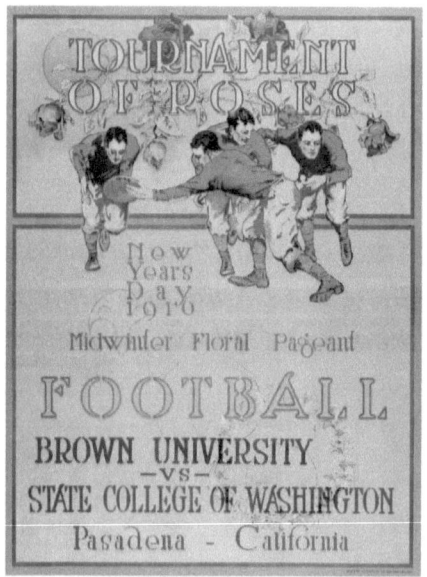

Traveling first class on a Pullman car required the players and coaches to live together in close quarters. Though Fritz Pollard had initially been resented by some of his teammates because of his race that was no longer an issue. Pollard had proved himself on the gridiron as a player, and in his relationships with the players as a good guy. Paradoxically, the problem was with the Black porters who serviced the Pullman car where the players slept, and in the dining car where they served meals. The porters served other players but not Pollard. Somewhat protectively the players made sure the star player was always fed. They would bring him food and drink. Why the Black porters acted this way was not altogether clear, but one thing was more than clarified. As a Black player, Pollard would all too often endure racial slights throughout his collegiate and professional football careers.

On December 27, 1915 the sun was out, shining brightly as advertised by the Chamber of Commerce and the Rose Bowl Committee. The Southern Pacific locomotive pulled slowly into Los Angeles. The trek across America was over. Basking in the warmth of Southern California the Brown University players were escorted by bus to the Hotel Raymond in Pasadena. A graduate of Harvard University owned the place. That was Walter Raymond. He was prepared to welcome his alma mater with an enthusiastic welcome. He did so with open arms and brown and white streamers everywhere in and around the hotel. He even had the property's trees decorated with miniature footballs.

Walter Raymond was a Boston native and the owner of a successful travel agency. He migrated to Southern California, there to build and run the most beautiful hotel of its day in Pasadena. His hotel was the first major hotel in the San Gabriel Valley. It catered to wealthy Easterners seeking escape from the snow and ice. Those who stayed in the hotel included such Hollywood stars as Charles Chaplin, Tom Mix, and Buster Keaton. President Teddy Roosevelt even paid a visit.

Unfortunately, the original hotel burned to the ground in 1895. Bearing the same name a new hotel was built in 1902-1903. It was even grander than the original. It had over 300 plush rooms. This was where the Brown football team would stay.

THE SECOND HOTEL RAYMOND   WALTER RAYMOND

The team checked into the hotel prepared to unpack, have a meal, and check out the practice schedule. All should have gone so smoothly. That was not to be. The desk clerk would not give Fritz Pollard a room, stating that he couldn't be accommodated. No mention was made of the player's race. None was needed. Again coming to the aid of their teammate the players put up a fuss, even indicating they would prefer other accommodations. They were prepared to go to another hotel. The coaches stepped in and resolved the issue behind closed doors. What exactly was said is unknown. In the end Pollard was given a room to himself somewhat secluded from his teammates. The hotel, it appears, would not bed a white player in the same room with a Black man. It appears that he was also asked to limit his presence in the hotel lobby.

The team practiced each day at Horace Mann School in preparation for the Rose Bowl. For those interested in trivia the school was named after the noted educator, who was a Brown

University graduate. Generally the players prepared for the game under a brilliant orb in the sky and warmish temperatures.

HORACE MANN

Once established in the Hotel Raymond the team was "entertained lavishly." The players were taken to "the outstanding places in Pasadena" as Pollard later recalled. As might be expected the team was taken to the major movie studios where they met the stars of the day. Impromptu entertainment included the players eluding the curfew hours established by the coaches. The players discovered a side elevator permitting them to leave and return with impunity. So to speak, young men, even those from the Ivy League, would be young men. But they were also football players, determined to showcase the strength of Ivy League Football. They were prepared to take on the players from some place called Pullman, Washington.

BROWN UNIVERSITY FOOTBALL TEAM   - 1 9 1 5
TOURNAMENT OF ROSES GAME PARTICIPANTS NEW YEARS DAY - 1916
BROWN   VERSUS WASHINGTON STATE

CHAPTER 2 – A ROSE BOWL PARADE

JANUARY 1, 1910

The Rose Bowl Parade always has a Grand Marshall. In 1910 it was Charles Frederick Holder, a businessman, noted sportsman, and an avid conservationist. He was the son of a wealthy Massachusetts Quaker family. The family provided for private schools that eventually led to a stint at the US Naval Academy. Rather than making the Navy a career Holder became a passionate naturalist and wrote many books on marine zoology and big-game fishing. He was also something of an anthropologist. He teamed with Russell Burnham in uncovering Mayan artifacts in Mexico. The discovery brought him some notoriety. The inscribed stone was found in the Valley of the Yaqui, Mexico. Legend has it that the stone fell down from the heavens ages ago and that the carving was done by human hands. It was sort of a Western Hemisphere "Rosetta Stone."

BURNHAM AND HOLDER

After a career as the curator of New York's American Museum of Natural History, Holder packed his bags and headed for Pasadena, California. In addition to his work as a philanthropist he founded the Tuna Club of Avalon on Santa Catalina Island. That was the impetus for his effort to properly manage the game fish in the nearby waters. Of course, what does all this have to do with a Rose Bowl Game?

In 1890, he was made the President of the Tournament of Roses Association. He held the job for two significant years. Along with others, plans were made to promote a Tournament of Roses parade on New Year's Day. Hopefully, visitors from the chilly East would flock to sunny Pasadena to attend the parade. This would be good for business, tourism, and the general economy. Why roses? Very simply, these beautiful flowers would be in bloom.

CHARLES HOLDER

The planned parade would include many carriages decorated with roses and every manner of flower. Local citizens would participate in constructing these first floats and driving them in the parade. Initially, no football game was scheduled. Instead, foot races were staged and later races by chariots and bicycles. There were even tug-of-war matches, along with jousting competitions. Though people turned out for the parade the other activities generated little crowd attraction. Something more was needed.

AN EARLY ROSE BOWL FLOAT

A CHARIOT RACE

A decision was made to host a football game. The game was originally entitled a Tournament East-West Football Game. The best team east of the Mississippi would play a team from the West. Hopefully, the game would attract fans and begin a tradition of a New Year's Bowl game.

JANUARY 1, 1902

The University of Michigan Wolverines was invited to represent the East. The Midwest players had gone undefeated, 10 - 0 and were known as the "Point-a-Minute" team. Unbelievably, they had scored 501 points on the opposition and no team had scored on them. Most football fans considered the team the national champions. Stanford University was chosen to represent the West. By comparison Stanford's record was lackluster: 3 – 1 -1. The new president of the Tournament of Roses was James Wagner. He guaranteed each team $3500 to cover the expenses and hoped for a reasonable profit based on a good turnout of fans. In the end 8,500 attended the game and a $3,161.86 profit was in the Tournament's till. The price of admission was $.50 to a dollar. An additional $1.00 was charged to bring a horse and buggy to the grounds.

The Michigan team rode in the Rose Parade in new uniforms and waving colorful school banners. Joyously the sun was out. The temperature was about 80 degrees. This was a far cry from the freezing temperatures and six inches of snow they had left behind. Inadvertently, the city had festooned the parade route with blue and gold banners. These happened to be the Michigan colors. The Stanford team was not amused.

THE 1902 MICHIGAN TEAM

As to the game…It wasn't played in the present Rose Bowl. It wouldn't be built until 1923. It was played in Tournament Park located at the corner of California Street and Wilson Avenue. It was known as the "town lot" before being renamed in 1900. Today the area is now a private park maintained by the California Institute of Technology in Pasadena.

TOURNAMENT FIELD

The game started at 2:57 p.m. For the first 30 minutes (what we would call the first two quarters) the suspect Stanford team proved stouter than Michigan anticipated. The "point-a-minute" guys from the Midwest held a precarious 17 – 0 lead at halftime. In the second half the boys from Palo Alto crumbled. The Wolverines literally scored at will. The final score was 49 to 0. The Stanford Indians had been scalped. Unknown to many the Stanford coach actually asked the Michigan team to end the game with eight minutes left. Taking mercy on the conceding opposition the victorious Michigan team agreed.

THE 1902 STANFORD TEAM

For those who love football trivia…

- the playing field was 110 yards long.
- touchdowns counted for 5 points.
- field goals were worth 5 points.
- the game was divided into two 30-minute halves.
- you needed to make 5-yards in 3 downs to make a first down.
- forward passes were not allowed.
- there were few substitutions.

Given the lopsided score the Tournament of Roses Committee decided to end the football experiment. The game seemed unappealing for any future effort. It was back to chariot races. The first Rose Bowl Game was now history. Thirteen years would pass before the next Rose Bowl Game would be played in 1916 with two new teams, the Washington State Cougars and the University of Brown Bears led by Fritz Pollard.

FRITZ

THE FIRST QUARTER

Football is like life. It requires perseverance, self-denial, hard work, sacrifice, dedication, and respect for authority.

Vince Lombardi, Football Coach

––––––––––

THE 1916 ROSE BOWL GAME

The powerful Easterners threatened first. Using line plungers from its double-wing formation the Brown team drove to the Washington State four-yard line before being stopped. The opposition players dug their heels into the mud and held off a Brown touchdown. Still, the favored team from the east had dominated in the early minutes. Could they keep it up? Later in the quarter Fritz Pollard intercepted a pass on his 25-yard line to stymie the Cougar advance. Brown's offense consisted mainly of end runs while Washington State ran line plunges. On punt returns Pollard proved shifty and slippery, eluding tacklers but in the end he was not able to escape the grasp of the Cougar players. Neither team was able to score in the first quarter. This was partially due to the drenched field that was now muddy and difficult to run on.

THE MUDDY FIELD

CHAPTER 3 – COLLEGE BOUND

Fritz Pollard enrolled in Brown University in 1915. Sibling pressure and parental nudging motivated this decision. The school was founded in 1764 in Providence, Rhode Island. It was the seventh-oldest institution of higher education in the United States. Brown was one of the first colleges to codify in its charter that "admission and instruction of students was to be equal regardless of their religious affiliation." That progressive attitude did not fully apply to racial affiliation. The private Ivy League school had about 1,000 students in 1915. Pollard enrolled at a time when there were less than 2,000 students in Black colleges across the country. There were fewer than fifty Blacks in predominately white institutions. Only two Black students were on the Brown campus, even though it had a tradition of admitting a few minorities each year. Over time two of them became famous: John Hope, who became the President of Morehouse College and William E.B. DuBois, who was a founding member of the National Association for the Advancement of Colored People (NAACP).

WILLIAM E.B. DUBOIS   JOHN HOPE

Pollard quickly ran into embedded racial attitudes on the Brown campus. He was excluded from joining fraternities and from participation in some school activities. Though he could live on campus he had to do so alone. No white student would room with him. The campus humor magazine, *The Brownian,* included racist cartoons of Blacks as it perpetuated racial stereotypes. Pollard quickly learned that he was accepted grudgingly and with limitations. Acceptance based on equality was still a distant dream. As long as he minded his own business and kept a low profile things were okay. He had learned the lessons of Jack Johnson, the heavyweight boxer who resisted the racist attitudes of his day. What was the lesson? Stay out of the way of the white man.

Pollard did satisfactory in his academic classes, but it was on the football field where he excelled. To do so he would have to prove his worth to Coach Edward N. Robinson. His coach had played halfback at Brown, 1892-1895. He was an outstanding athlete. He won nine letters in football, baseball and track. After graduation he earned a law degree at Boston University. He then applied himself to coaching with stints at Nebraska, Brown, and Tufts. Overall his coaching record was 140 - 82 - 12. He coached the most victories in Brown history.

COACH ROBINSON

Coach Edward North Robinson has been called the "father of Brown football." He did so at a time when Eastern football was considered the best in the nation. His teams were generally undermanned yet very competitive against the gridiron powers of his day, Yale and Harvard in particular.

As a coach he stressed fundamentals, particularly precise blocking and sure tackling. His practices included what was called Bloody Wednesday. This was a tough scrimmage to decide who would start on game day. Robinson wanted to know who could play talent-wise, but also who was motivated to fight for a starting position. That view extended to scrubs, including Pollard. The coach was open to playing a Black if he could prove himself. Young Pollard was determined to do so even though many Brown players resented him. That resentment played out in many ways. The player wouldn't shower with him. Many wouldn't sit next to him or near him on the trolley that took players from the practice field to the campus. On the practice field there were extra hits on the slim running back when he was tackled. The players would pile on him to make him quit. He wouldn't. He would get up and smile. He wouldn't retaliate no matter the provocation. Whatever anger he felt he kept to himself. All this the rookie player endured. Slowly, however, he was accepted by his teammates for his football prowess and as a good person. One story illustrates this.

Wallace Wade was a teammate of Pollard. When Wade's father found out that a Black was on the team he demanded that his son leave the university. Young Wade and Fritz had become pals. Though it was difficult the son stood up to his father, describing his friend as a "good person and teammate." He pointed out that Fritz was a "good chap" and that they took their meals together at the training table. At this point Coach Robinson stepped into the fray and helped convince the father to relent. He did. Years later Wallace Wade, having learned the coaching basics at Brown, went on to successfully coach at Alabama and Duke. At Alabama his record was 61 – 13 – 3. This included three national championship teams, 1925, 1926, and 1930. At Duke it was 110 – 36 – 7. He was also 2 – 0 – 1 in Rose Bowl games. He coached for 40 years. In 1955 he was inducted into the College Hall of Fame. He was credited with making the Crimson Tide into a major football power.

WALLACE WADE

It's not often that a football coach makes the cover of *Time Magazine*. Wade did so on October 25, 1937. It should also be noted that he served in two world wars in the artillery.

In time Pollard won his place on the team. He was fleet-footed. He ran low and fast, and was elusive. Soon he was dubbed the "human torpedo." In time the players no longer shunned him. He was now accepted as the only Black player on the Brown football team. It should also be noted that he was the only Black player in the Ivy League schools in 1915.

MAKING THE TEAM – 1915

The 1915 Yale-Brown game proved to be the turning point in Pollard's career. The game was played in the newly constructed Yale Bowl in New Haven, Connecticut. It was approximately 70-miles from Rhode Island and less than 2-miles from the Yale Campus. The Yale Bowl was a marvel of its day when it opened in 1914. It could seat 70,000 plus fans. It was designed by Charles Ferry and would later inspire the construction of the Los Angeles Memorial Coliseum, the Rose Bowl in Pasadena, and the Michigan University Stadium in Ann Arbor. It would be declared a National Historic Landmark in 1987. Curiously, no locker rooms or restrooms were included in the construction for the players. They had to dress in the Smilow Field Centre and walk 200 yards to the field. Apparently the home team liked that since Yale fans could cheer them on as they walked. Of course, the same fans could jeer the opposing team. The first game was played in the Yale Bowl on November 21, 1914, a year before Pollard made his name on the Bulldog turf.

THE YALE BOWL

Going into the game Brown was considered the underdog to "the mighty Blue of Yale." Though not having a great year Yale was the elite of college football at that time. Brown's football program was considered second rate. However, the feisty Brown team felt confident it could win. Over 350 fans felt the same way. They took a separate train to the game.

The Brown team entered the field, minus one player. Because of threats and in order to avoid violence, Pollard took a separate entrance. He came on the field just before the kickoff. Once on the field he heard painful, racist chants. "Catch the Nig--r" "Kill the Nig--r" and "Bye, Bye Black Birdie." On the field Pollard had a great game returning long punts, and proving to be fast, elusive, and difficult to tackle. The Black newspaper, the *New York Age*, stated that:

Pollard gained more ground than any other Brown player. His end run of thirty yards featured the third period, while his catching of punts and his clever fast run backs held Brown safe after its lead of three points had been secured.

Brown defeated Yale, 3 – 0. This win was only the second time in their previous twenty-three meetings since 1880. Fritz emerged from the game as "a budding star in college football," or at least in New England. This honor even included a Yale lineman who approached the Brown back after the game. As the story goes the Yale player said, "You're a nig--r, but you're the best goddam football player I ever saw."

CARRYING THE BALL FOR BROWN

The triumph over Yale led to a joyous return to Providence. A large crowd of Brown partisans greeted the team. Many of those fans were appraised of the game by telegraph, or by microphone from the *Providence Journal Building.* Radio coverage was not yet in vogue. Brown fans were ecstatic and Pollard was becoming a sports celebrity in the Black press.

CHAPTER 4 – A UNIQUE FAMILY

As the Pullman car bearing the Brown football team headed to Pasadena, we can speculate that Fritz Pollard mused about his family and perhaps anticipated the futures of his siblings.

Fritz Pollard was born on January 27, 1894. He would live for 92 years, dying on May 11, 1986. His birth certificate indicates he was named Frederick Douglas Pollard in honor of the famous abolitionist. In the family household he was called Fred. Many of the neighborhood kids were of German abstraction and referred to him as Fritz. The nickname stuck.

FRITZ POLLARD   FREDERICK DOUGLAS

Fritz's father was John William Pollard (1846 – 1932). He was born in Virginia during slave days. His mother feared for his safety and that of his sisters who were not yet tenured to the odious practice. Pro-slavery zealots were kidnapping and selling Black children into bondage. To avoid this she took her children to Kansas to be raised and educated. This was when the state was caught up in its own mini-civil war, sometimes described as the time of "Bleeding Kansas." Once the South seceded John Pollard joined the 2nd Colored Kansas Regiment. He distinguished himself in a number of skirmishes. Following the war he was encouraged by two Black US Senators to continue his education. Both men were from Mississippi and held office during the Reconstruction Period. Apparently, John Pollard wanted to attend Oberlin College in Ohio. Noted for its progressive policies the college accepted both Blacks and women. A bout with smallpox derailed going to Oberlin and ended his desire to be an attorney. Needing to earn his way he learned the barber trade from a white man. In this trade he became a master barber. This reputation always served him well within the white community with a large clientele of men in need of a close shave and an attractive haircut. In time he moved to Mexico, Missouri to ply his trade. There he would meet and marry Catherine Amanda Hughes (1856 – 1937).

Fritz's mother was born in Middleton, Missouri. Her DNA was off the wall, so to speak. She was Black, Sioux, and of French descent. She was well educated for her time. She married John Pollard and within a short span they had three children: Artissmisia, Luther J. and Willie Naoimi. It appears she was ahead of her time. She was strong-willed, a successful seamstress, and a staunch supporter of education. Juggling both home and work she was a demanding, tough love mother with high expectations for her children. She was also aware of racial prejudice and the potential for violence against her family. Family lore suggests she never answered the front door without a pistol in her apron pocket. As showed by tax documents checks signed by her, she played a firm role in the family's finances.

THE POLLARDS

In 1886, racial tensions were increasing in Missouri. Always protective of her family Fritz's mother encouraged a move to Illinois, both for safety and for greater educational opportunities. Inexplicably the family moved to the Village of Rogers Park, a small town just outside of Chicago. At the time this was an all-white community. Somehow the family fit in as a respectable household. They settled in at 1928 Lunt Avenue long before the area would be annexed by the city of Chicago in 1896. John Pollard set up his barbershop at 7017 East Ravenswood Avenue, which was then located in the Evanston Township. One can speculate that the need for a master barber paved the way for the modest integration of the area. The Pollards were the only Black family in the community. In this new home additional children found their way into the world: Leslie, Hughes, Ruth Pollard, and Fritz. In any event the family was not confined to a ghetto. The children were raised within a white community and would attend school within Rogers Park. In this they were most fortunate.

THE LUNT AVENUE HOME

All families have a history. Without question the Pollard family distinguished itself during a period when it was difficult for Blacks to advance. Artemisia Pollard (1875 – 1961) attended Brown University and earned a degree in nursing. She became the first Black registered nurse in Illinois.

Luther Pollard (1878 – 1977) was an all-star athlete in high school, doing well in both football and baseball. His ambition was to play professional baseball. This goal was stymied by the "unwritten agreement" to ban Blacks from the game. His efforts to describe himself as Native-American failed. Thwarted in this effort he became a life and accident insurance agent after first attending Dartmouth College, where he played on the football team. In later years, he founded a picture production company called the Ebony Film Corporation. This was the first motion picture company to use an all-Black cast. The company was actually controlled by whites. They had provided the funding. It was rumored that Luther was hired to give a Black face to the company as the president and general manager. Unfortunately, racist white investors only wanted to exploit Black audiences. Regardless of this Luther worked to end Black stereotypes within the company's films: no crap shooting, no razors or knifes, no stealing chickens, and knock off the watermelon bit. He also tried to showcase Black talent. He was not altogether successful in these endeavors. The comedy films were both praised and condemned for their stereotyping of Blacks. Without question Fritz Pollard looked up to his older brother as an inspiring role model.

LUTHER POLLARD

Naomi Pollard (1883 – 1971) was the first Black woman to graduate from Northwestern University. Though she excelled in her studies she was denied election to Phi Beta Kappa because of her race. She became a school teacher. She later attended the University of Chicago to gain her librarian certificate. She practiced this profession in the Chicago Public Library System. With her husband, Dr. Richard Dobson, she moved to Sioux City, Iowa where she was involved in the NAACP and the League of Women Voters. Eventually she became a professor of education at Wilberforce University in Ohio.

NAOMI POLLARD HUGHES POLLARD

Hughes Pollard (1891 – 1926) had a musical career, most notably as a drummer with the Melody Four in Chicago. This jazz group toured in Europe and Australia. During World War I he joined the French army. After the war he formed his own orchestra that combined the talents of European and American jazz players. He died a few years later in Chicago of complications from a mustard gas attack in France.

Leslie Pollard (1888 – 1915) was considered the most outstanding athlete in a family of great athletes. He played baseball and football at North Division High School and later attended Dartmouth College where he played football for one season. He was called the "Black whirlwind" by the *New York Age* newspaper. Over the years he was a sports writer in New York City as well as the First Secretary of the Urban League in the city. He also coached football for a few seasons at Lincoln University in Pennsylvania. Tragically, he died of asphyxiation from carbon monoxide gas while living in Brooklyn, New York. He was only 27-years of age.

LESLIE POLLARD

Ruth Pollard did not have the celebrity status of her siblings (1889 – 1941). She was a track athlete at Lake View High School. She was a stenographer and lived in the Pollard residence for her entire life. Little else is known about her.

Prompted by their educated-minded parents all the Pollard children graduated from high school. In the case of Fritz Pollard that meant Albert G. Lane Technical School, located near Chicago. When the school opened in 1908 it was the first large manual training school in the United States with an enrollment of 1800 students. Fritz Pollard was a member of the first graduating class. Over the years others would join the school's famous alumni: Edgar Bergan, the ventriloquist and buddy of Charlie McCarthy; Frankie Lane, the singer; Johnny Weissmuller, the Olympic swimmer and Tarzan's best friend, and John Podesta, the Chief of Staff for President Bill Clinton.

ALBERT G. LANE TECHNICAL SCHOOL

While in the school, he took a variety of vocational classes, including blacksmithing, foundry work, and pattern skills. His academic studies included English, algebra, chemistry, and foreign language. His extra curricula endeavors revolved around playing the trombone in the school's orchestra, participating on the debate team, and of course, playing football and baseball, when not sprinting on the track. He graduated in 1912. On October 1, 2022, some 110 years later, the City of Chicago and Cook County made that date the "Fritz Pollard Day." Four bronze plaques were unveiled at the high school, each of which chronicled the achievements of Fritz Pollard, including his time at Lane High, his football days at Brown University, his playing and coaching in professional football, and his efforts in business to bring about greater social justice. In remembering Fritz the school lived out its own motto: "Wherever You Go, Whatever You Do, Remember the Honor of Lane."

While playing football at Lane Fritz Pollard's older brothers taught him survival strategies to be used on and off the field. Because of his small stature, 5'8" and weighing only 170 pounds, he was a popular target for bigger guys who wanted to tackle the speedy and elusive Black runner. Teams gang tackled him on kickoffs and pounded him into the turf. Where latent racial feelings existed tacklers seemed to hit Fritz with extra zest. This was especially true on wet and muddy fields where tacklers pushed his face into pools of water. His older brothers taught him to run close to the ground and to dip even more so when about to be hit. When tackled they taught him to lie on his back face up and to pump his legs fast as if he were riding a bicycle. This kept the opponents from piling on. And no matter how hard he was hit to get up quickly and with a hint of a smile suggesting he could take the punishment. The lessons he learned on the high school football field sustained him on the college gridiron and in professional football.

As to the off field lessons taught by his role model brothers...
Pollard was taught that athletic success was possible. He was
also taught how to handle it. Don't show off. Don't embarrass
or threaten the white players. Play tough but within the rules.
The white press, he was told, could accept a Black champion, but
not one that called into question the dignity of the white man.
He was taught that there was an unwritten code of conduct.
You could be aggressive but there were limitations. He couldn't
always fight back. He had to choose his fights. Over time he saw
the wisdom of their mentoring, especially when it came to Jack
Johnson's story as related to him by his older brothers.

On December 26, 1908 Johnson defeated Tommy Burns, the
Canadian boxing champion, for the heavyweight championship
of the world. Johnson would hold the title for thirteen years. In
doing so he became the most famous Black boxer, if not the most
notorious Black athlete in the world. No one questioned his
skills in the ring. What got him into trouble during Jim Crow
times with an antagonistic white press was the way he flaunted
the racist norms of the day. Johnson dated white women, one
of whom he married. He opened a desegregated restaurant
and nightclub with his wife. He wore flashy clothes and drove
expensive cars. In a way he was living the white man's dream
life.

In some quarters Johnson became a symbol of Black rebellion
against a segregated society that discriminated against those of
color. He challenged all those who would keep the Black man
in his place. Success in the ring permitted him to say, "You
can't control me." All of this came to a head on July 4, 1910. Jim
Jefferies fought and lost in a heavyweight brawl with Johnson.
Jefferies had been labeled the "white man's hope," a fighter

who could grab Johnson's championship belt. Unfortunately, Johnson's victory set off widespread rioting around the country. Though Blacks were jubilant in victory they were also victims in the aftermath of the fight.

The older brothers drummed into their youthful sibling at least three lessons. First, athletic success was possible. This was also true in business. Second, handle success carefully. Don't show off. Third, don't threaten the white man. Taken together the pitch was this. You live in a white world and must accommodate yourself to it in order to survive. These lessons sustained Fritz Pollard throughout his life.

Once in Pasadena Fritz Pollard had a few moments to consider how his football team got to California, as well as his first year at Brown University. The team's record was nothing to yell about. The first three games in 1915 were painful losses to Amherst (7 – 0), Syracuse (17 – 7), and Harvard (17 – 7). The fourth game was a 0 – 0 tie with Trinity. At that point the season was in disarray. Then things turned around. There were victories over Rhode Island (38 – 0), Williams (33 – 0), Vermont (46 – 0), Yale (3 – 0), and Carlisle (39 – 3). By the end of the season the Brown Bears were a competitive team. The season was salvaged and over. No bowl invitation was offered for one simple reason. There were no bowl games.

Out west, however, consideration was being given to resurrecting a game in Pasadena. Sometime in 1915 the Rose Bowl Committee agreed to invite teams, again one from the East, one from the West. Offers were made to Michigan and Syracuse. They were quickly declined. Yale chose not to play in the post-season game. Almost by default Brown was offered an invitation. The players voted to play. The school administration agreed.

Washington State College was not the Rose Bowl Committee's first choice. Initially, the University of Washington was invited. The school administration, however, declined the offer, feeling that academics came before athletics. That being the case Washington State was asked to play in the Rose Bowl in what would later be called "the granddaddy of all bowl games." The school accepted. Though a bridesmaid the Cougars were an undefeated team with a chip on their shoulders. They wanted to prove that they were as good as their record and that they could compete with the powerful eastern teams.

28 – 3 over Oregon
29 – 0 over Oregon State
41 – 0 over Idaho
27 – 7 over Montana
17 – 0 over Whitman
48 – 0 over Gonzaga

THE 1915 WASHINGTON STATE TEAM

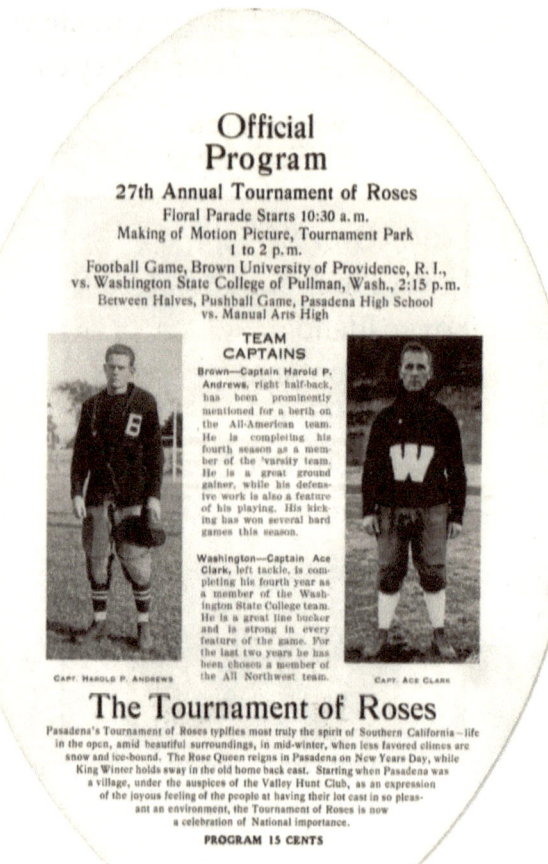

Official
Program

27th Annual Tournament of Roses

Floral Parade Starts 10:30 a.m.
Making of Motion Picture, Tournament Park
1 to 2 p.m.
Football Game, Brown University of Providence, R. I.,
vs. Washington State College of Pullman, Wash., 2:15 p.m.
Between Halves, Pushball Game, Pasadena High School
vs. Manual Arts High

TEAM CAPTAINS

Brown—Captain Harold P. Andrews, right half-back, has been prominently mentioned for a berth on the All-American team. He is completing his fourth season as a member of the 'varsity team. He is a great ground gainer, while his defensive work is also a feature of his playing. His kicking has won several hard games this season.

Washington—Captain Ace Clark, left tackle, is completing his fourth year as a member of the Washington State College team. He is a great line bucker and is strong in every feature of the game. For the last two years he has been chosen a member of the All Northwest team.

CAPT. HAROLD P. ANDREWS   CAPT. ACE CLARK

The Tournament of Roses

Pasadena's Tournament of Roses typifies most truly the spirit of Southern California — life in the open, amid beautiful surroundings, in mid-winter, when less favored climes are snow and ice-bound. The Rose Queen reigns in Pasadena on New Years Day, while King Winter holds sway in the old home back east. Starting when Pasadena was a village, under the auspices of the Valley Hunt Club, as an expression of the joyous feeling of the people at having their lot cast in so pleasant an environment, the Tournament of Roses is now a celebration of National importance.

PROGRAM 15 CENTS

1641

Fritz Pollard was going to the Rose Bowl. He would be the only Black player on either team. The 1915 season had been good for him, but not necessarily for Blacks in America. A few examples follow.

Woodrow Wilson was in the White House having won the 1912 presidential election. He was the first Southerner since the Civil War to achieve this high station. As a child of the South he had sympathies for both segregationist policies and for the "Lost Cause." These views ran counter to Washington

D.C. where 10% of the federal workforce was Black and a flourishing Black middle class population existed in the city. Overall, Blacks comprised almost 30% of the capital's citizens. True the city's neighborhoods suffered from racist attitudes leading to segregation in public and private institutions. Still, the federal government was integrated since Reconstruction Days. Wilson changed all that. He gave his newly appointed cabinet the permission to segregate their departments, to limit the hiring of Blacks, as well as their promotions. Critics, of course, cried foul, pointing out that these policies were racist, humiliating and degrading, and entirely unwarranted. Wilson did not relent.

PRESIDENT WILSON

In 1915 the President went to the movies. He and his family had a private screening of D.W. Griffith's new film, *Birth of a Nation*. The film was an adaptation of Thomas Dixon's *The Clansman,* a novel that gave a historically inaccurate history of the Reconstruction Era in American history (1865 – 1876). The film depicted the Northern States (the Union) as aggressors who invaded the South. It also glorified the Ku Klux Klan (KKK) as saviors of the South or what some called "redeemers." The KKK was depicted as a heroic force attempting to preserve American values, while protecting white women and maintaining white supremacy in the defeated Confederacy. In particular the film portrayed Blacks as lacking intelligence and sexually aggressive toward white women. The film emphasized the worst racist views about Blacks and contributed to discriminatory and segregationist policies. Simply put, it inflamed racial tensions. After screening the film the President supposedly said, "The film was like writing history with lightning. My only regret is that it is all so terribly true." His words lent credence to this racist and false understanding of the post-Civil War period.

The great migration of thousands of Blacks from the Southern states to the North was also arousing racial tensions. Blacks were competing with whites for jobs and housing in order to improve their lives. Integration was running headlong into segregationist attitudes. It would be no different in the world of athletics.

This was the world Pollard inherited as he entered Brown University in 1915 and played in the Rose Bowl the next year.

THE SECOND QUARTER

The difference between a successful person and others is not a lack of strength, not a lack of knowledge, but rather a lack of will.

Vince Lombardi, Football Coach

What we would call the second quarter began well for the Brown team. The Bears drove down to the Washington State's 12-yard line. The team had first and ten and high hopes. Strong line smashes appeared to make a touchdown all but inevitable. A pass interception ended that. The Cougar quarterback called wide end runs to begin their own drive. That was Art "Bull" Durham. The end runs proved ineffective. The Bears were ready. John Butner and Josh Weeks burst through the interference and downed the runners from the Northwest. Unfortunately, both men were hurt and couldn't play in the second half. Late in the period Brown once more advanced deep into Washington State's territory. Using line bucks by H.P. Andrews and C.J. Purdy, and a 10-yard run by Pollard the Brown team appeared ready to score. Once again the team bogged down. The teams had successfully fought to a 0 – 0 tie by halftime. The muddy field had silenced touchdowns.

CHAPTER 6 – THE UNUSUAL COACH

It was a cold, crisp day with cloudy skies and the threat of snow flurries in the nearby mountains. The Washington State football team, bedecked in school colors, quickly boarded the Portland Flyer for a train trip of less than a 1,000 miles to Pasadena, California. The players did so after a fancy send-off dinner at Spokane's Davenport Hotel. According to plan the team would arrive in Pasadena on Christmas morning. It did. As advertised by the Chamber of Commerce the sun was a brilliant ball in the sky, warming those at the Santa Monica beaches and others strolling through Griffith Park and the streets of Hollywood. There was no obvious forecast for a change in the weather. The Rose Bowl would be played in ideal football weather.

An unusual present awaited the team, one arranged by their coach, William Henry "Lone Star" Dietz. Though known as a taskmaster on the practice field, the coach had signed his players up to be in a Hollywood movie. Unbelievably the Cougars would portray a fictional football team in the movie called *Tom Brown of Harvard*. Each player would make $100 for 14 days of work. Not bad for student-athletes of that day. When not on the set, of course, the players had to participate in twice-a-day practices. The players would earn their money.

COACH DIETZ

The film was based on a 1906 Broadway play entitle *Brown of Harvard*. The plot line was a bit confusing but very intriguing. Tom Brown was a student at Harvard. He was also a football player. He was engaged to Evelyn Ames. Her brother was Wilton Ames. He was involved with Marian Thorne. As the plot line goes Marian was pregnant. The stigma for Marian's condition was unfairly placed on Tom Brown by Wilton. This rascal also borrowed money from Tom and forged a check for $300 from his account. Wilton used the money to get Marian out of town before her pregnancy was known far and wide. Evelyn, of course, believed that Tom was behind all of this and broke off her engagement with the poor guy. She also thought he should marry Marian. He needed to make a decent woman out of her. Eventually Wilton's nefarious acts came to light and he confessed to all. Tom was now off the hook. Reconciliation followed and Tom and Evelyn got on with their lives. Though the plot left much to be desired the players enjoyed their work and appreciated the money.

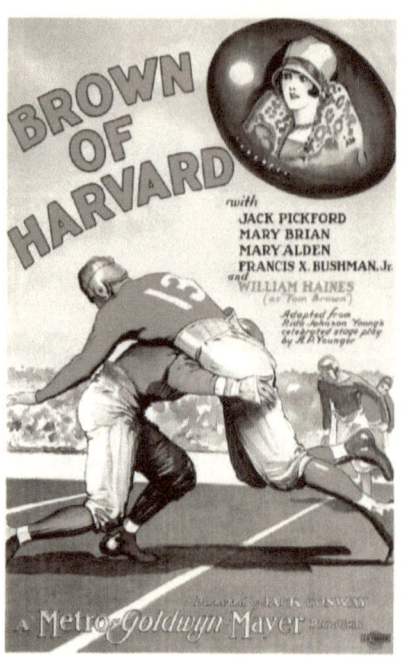

The film was released in 1918 two years after the second Rose Bowl pitting the Bears of Brown University against the Cougars of Washington State. As to which was better, the movie or the game, that is still a matter of conjecture.

Coach Dietz was quite a guy. He was born on August 17, 1884 in Rice Lake, Wisconsin. His father was the local county sheriff and considered a pretty tough guy. That characteristic rubbed off on his son. In time Dietz played football at the Carlisle Indian School in Pennsylvania, 1902 - 1903. He played tackle and opened up holes for the legendary Jim Thorpe. The coach of the team was the equally famous Glenn Scobey "Pop" Warner. He was responsible for several innovations including the single and double wing formations that were precursors of the modern spread and shotgun strategies. He also initiated the three-point stance and body blocking techniques. Besides developing an elite program at Carlisle he coached teams to four national championships: Pittsburgh in 1915, 1916, and 1918, and Stanford in 1926. The guy was a winner.

No question about it. Playing with these guys inspired Dietz's football skills and later coaching acumen. After Carlisle he continued his studies at Macalester College in Saint Paul, Minnesota before beginning a long coaching career that eventually took him to a land grant school in Pullman, Washington, WSC (1915 – 1917) His two year record there was 17 – 2 – 1. Later he would coach at Louisiana Tech and Wyoming. His college coaching record was 103 – 59 – 7. He ended up coaching in the pro ranks for the Boston Redskins in the nascent National Football League, 1933 – 1934. His record was 11 – 11 – 2. In 2012, he was inducted into the College Football Hall of Fame as a coach. Not bad for a guy from Rice Lake, Wisconsin.

WILLIAM DIETZ   JIM THORPE   POP WARNER

Dietz emphasized conditioning. He inherited players at WSC who needed stamina and endurance when players often played both offense and defense. When he took over he had only a few experienced players and lots of untested guys. Almost all were unfamiliar with the single or double wing formations he brought to Pullman. These he had learned from Pop Warner. In preparing for the Rose Bowl he concentrated on stopping Fritz Pollard. Controlling him was the key to winning the game. That mantra he hammered into his team. Privately he told each player the same thing: "I'm counting on you to do the job." He also fathered a rumor that he was quitting after the game, especially if the Cougars were licked. He assumed the players were determined to keep their coach. They would play to win.

A few days before the game the unthinkable occurred. The skies clouded. Temperatures fell. Then the rain started, slowly at first and then pelting the sunny land of oranges, lemons, and grapefruit. In the last days before the game 3-inches of snow fell in the nearby San Gabriel Mountains and rain poured without stop from the heavens, then slackened, but the damage was done. The Tournament Field venue quickly became a muddy field with lots of puddles. Taking stock of this, Dietz changed his game strategy. He decided to avoid running a wide-open offense with lots of tricky ball handing. He knew the ball would be wet and slippery. He shifted to cautious running plays and line-bucks against the larger Brown line. This would be a game fought in the trenches.

The day of the game the Rose Parade began at 10:30 a.m. in a light drizzle. The carriages and cars paraded down Orange Blvd. And then the rain came in heaps. It was the first time in twenty-four years that it rained on New Year's Day. The parade, however, was a success, though over a little faster than usual. The dampness actually helped the rose-decked floats. The spectators along the route were damp but delighted.

Dietz's strategy paid off. By game time Tournament Park was a bloody mess. The weather conditions favored the Cougars. They were wearing cleats for a muddy field. Accepting the Chamber of Commerce reports about sunny Southern California, the Brown team left their wet cleats in Rhode Island. Dry weather cleats allowed you start fast, cut, and run faster, all virtues ascribed to Pollard. Without wet-weather cleats it was difficult to get traction. Pollard was neutralized. He felt like he was anchored to the mud and to some rough play. On one particular play he was tackled and fell to the ground, face first into a 4-inch puddle. The opposition took its time getting off him, leaving him gasping for breath. Coach Robinson pulled him off the field to protect his star running back. Hopping up and down Pollard resisted his coach, but to no avail. Apparently Walt Disney was at the game and saw Pollard's protesting. Much later he included the runner's antics in a Mickey Mouse cartoon. Whether Pollard ever saw the cartoon is unknown.

Some trivia…With 8,000 rain-soaked fans, many with umbrellas, in attendance neither team was able to get anything going in the first half. Tickets had sold for 50 cents to a buck. Each team was guaranteed $5,000. Ultimately, the Tournament of Roses sponsors lost $11,000 on the game.

Even before the game those covering the Rose Bowl suggested that neither team would play up to midseason form.

The reasoning was this. It would be difficult to keep the players interested in hard practices after the regular season closed following Thanksgiving Day. These pundits of the sport pointed out that the climate was very much different than Providence, Rhode Island, or Pullman, Washington. How that would affect practice was never spelled out. On one score these football observers were right on. The game plans of both teams would be negated if the weather turned bad. Each coach would then have to adapt to a sodden field. For its part the Tournament Park folks worked overtime to protect the field. It was covered with a tarpaulin and sawdust early in the morning of the game and that helped, at least through the first quarter. After that the field was a quagmire. If the first half were any indication a muddy standoff would continue in the second half.

PLAYING IN THE MUD

CHAPTER 7 – THE OTHER MOVIE

It is assumed the Brown players heard about the good luck of the Washington team's involvement with Hollywood. Meeting movie stars and earning money while being nicely fed on the film lot was enough to make the Easterners a bit jealous. Human nature being what it is this is more than conjecture. For one player in particular that memory led to something special. Many years later Fritz Pollard would produce a film in 1956. It was called *Rockin' the Blues*. It premiered at Harlem's famed Apollo Theater in October. What made the film special was this. The cast was Black. The film was aimed specifically at Black audiences at a time when many movie houses were segregated into separate viewing sections and when Black artists seldom had roles beyond stereotypic images nurtured by Jim Crow prejudice.

Long after his collegiate and professional football career Pollard had achieved some notoriety in business. One of those ventures was Fritz Pollard Associates. He set up Austin Productions as a subsidiary of his company and raised $350,000 for the *Rockin' the Blues* project. He invested considerable personal funds into financing the film. He used a studio in the Bronx where earlier he had made film shorts called Soundies. His motivation for the enterprise was straight up. As in professional football and baseball and now in the entertainment industry, he wanted to end discriminatory practices that fell harshly on Blacks and other minorities. He wanted to prove that integration was possible on the playing field and on the movie set. He wanted everyone to have a fair opportunity to succeed. This was a lifetime quest on his part, which, it can be assumed, grew out of his own experiences with the pain of racist abuses. He wanted to end racism in all its ugly manifestations.

The film's plot had something to do with a camp show staged for Black soldiers during WWII. Music and comedy were at the heart of the film. It took advantage of the "rock and roll" craze sweeping the country. A major effort was made to introduce new talent to the public through musical revue. The film would launch the careers of Connie Carroll, the Miller Sisters, Pearl Woods, and Linda Hopkins. Many groups also got exposure, such as the Harptones and the Hurricanes.

THE HARPTONES   THE MILLER SISTERS

One member of the cast was well known to most Americans. Mantan Moreland was a veteran comedian, who was best known for his role as the bug-eyed chauffeur in the Charlie Chan movies. Who could forget his famous line when danger lurked and he wanted to escape: "Feet do yo' stuff."

MANTAN MORELAND

Pollard's film was a financial success, though not an artistic triumph. It did, however, jumpstart the careers of many fine Black entertainers. Pollard was much more than a football player. In his own way he was a civil rights activist long before the term was coined. He sought out and assisted young Black talent. He was a one-man agent for affirmative action.

PROMOTING YOUNG TALENT

CHAPTER 8 – THE SOUNDIES

Soundies were 3-minute American musical films. They were mainly produced between 1941-1946. Fritz Pollard was involved in this business. The short films have been called "precursors to music videos" that later played on television. These films exhibited a variety of musical genres in order to reach the widest audience possible. The short film productions were viewed on Panorams. These were coin operated 16mm rear projection machines.

The machines were located in nightclubs, bars, restaurants, taverns, pool halls, and factory lounges. Panorams were essentially a jukebox playing movies. The Mills Novelty Company of Chicago manufactured the machines. Each machine contained eight Soundies films. Each film was threaded through an endless-loop arrangement. A unique system of mirrors flashed the image from the lower half of the cabinet onto a front-facing screen in the top half. It cost ten cents to play a movie. There was no index to choose a certain film. The customer saw what was next in the mechanical queue. The films were changed each week. Lots of now famous people got their start with Soundies, including Duke Ellington, Dorothy Dandridge, Cab Calloway, Lena Horne, Nat King Cole, and Louis Armstrong. The Panorams showcased all of this Black talent and more. In a way the Soundies sidestepped discriminatory practices in the traditional music industry. Eventually about 1800 mini-musical Soundies were made. Very few exist today.

NAT KING COLE

DOROTHY DANDRIDGE

MILLS BROTHERS

The Soundies also included other celebrities in their earliest moments leading to stardom. The list includes Lawrence Welk, Doris Day, Ricardo Montalban, Gene Krupa, Liberace, Alan Ladd, and Marilyn Maxwell. That's quite a group.

ALAN LADD   DORIS DAY   RICARDO MONTALBAN

Given the array of talent played on a Panoram it would be nice to think that the Soundies industry was integrated. That was not the case. The Soundies were as segregated as the country. Black artists were listed under a special category on the Panorams. That made it easier for segregated facilities to determine what to play. Generally, the Soundies had an all-white or all-Black cast. There were only a few Latino performers and no Asians. One Soundie, however, was integrated: *Let Me Off Uptown*. It included Anita O'Day, Roy Eldridge, and Gene Krupa.

It's fair to ask how Fritz Pollard got into this business? The Mills Novelty Company made the Panoram cabinets. The company hired Pollard to manage their New York City office. Since he was already a talent agent for Black artists and had been involved in movie productions, he was an excellent choice. Under his guidance the musicians rehearsed their numbers at Pollard's Suntan Movie Studio in Harlem. Then the acts were shot in a Bronx studio he had an interest in. In many cases the performers recorded the music in advance and mimed in the soundtrack during the filming. The films were inexpensively made, sometimes within one day. The Soundies Distribution Corporation of America distributed the Soundies. Pollard had a hand in all aspects of the production process.

The Soundies Distributing Company was active until 1947. A number of factors led to its demise. The traditional movie houses felt challenged by this technology. Economic alarms went off in Hollywood. The proposed manufacturing of 100,000 Panoram machines was an existential threat to the established industry. In the end only 5,000 machines would be built. As might be expected the projectionist union members objected to the machines. No projectionist was needed. Some objected to the short films focusing on the crossing and recrossing of attractive female legs, or shots of bobbing breasts on the mini-screen. Compared to uptight Hollywood the Soundies were quite racy, especially when they included burlesque stars such as Sally Rand. The fact that men enjoyed the films was not lost on those producing the Soundies.

SALLY RAND

Two other challenges faced the upstart industry. Though the Soundies included wartime messages stressing patriotism and the purchase of war bonds, increasing war restrictions on materials used in making the Panoram machines cut into their production. The biggest threat, however, came from the emerging commercial television industry. Soundies films and machines were becoming obsolete. By 1948 the Panoram machines were junked. The film industry would move on, as would Pollard. The Soundies were an important part of Black cinema history, as well as Pollard's efforts to integrate movies. That was a legacy to be remembered.

HALFTIME

FOOTBALL IS A GAME PLAYED WITH ARMS, LEGS, AND SHOULDERS BUT MOSTLY FROM THE NECK UP.

Knute Rockne, Football Coach

———————

There are no known records of what was said in each locker room at halftime. Most probably bruises and injuries were to be attended to as quickly as possible. Thirst would be slackened. All players caught their breath and took a moment to rest. Each coach, it is thought, congratulated their respective players for staying tough in a rain drenched first half. Raising their voices a notch the two coaches pointed out errors in play and what needed to be fixed. Of course, one thing couldn't be fixed. The Cougars had cleats for the soggy field; the Bears didn't have them. The edge went to Washington State. Knowing this both coaches suggested how their game plans would have to be altered again because of the foul weather in light of the cleat issue. As would be expected the coaches ended the temporary locker room respite with motivational words... "Win one for Brown!" "Men of Washington, this is your moment." The players probably clasped hands and bellowed, "Let's do it!"

BATTLING IN THE MUD

CHAPTER 9 – EARNING A BUCK

Fritz Pollard had to work his way through college. Brown University could provide only modest assistance. There was no football scholarship. Though he came from a middleclass Black family finances were always tight in the Pollard home. That being the case Pollard had to be industrious and innovative in earning a buck. He was. He supplemented his finances by creating the "pressing club" at Brown. Each member paid $1.00 per month. For that paltry sum he was entitled to unlimited pressing and repairs. To do this Pollard turned his dormitory room into a mini-factory for the pressing equipment and for the storage of clothes. There was a curious aside to this entrepreneurial venture. Pollard always seemed to be well dressed for special occasions. The rumor was he wore clothes left in his safekeeping. One wonders if the actual owner ever saw his clothes dashing around the campus?

There was an interesting sidelight to this business. John D. Rockefeller, Jr. was an 1897 Brown graduate. After the 1915 football season he visited Pollard in his dorm room where he saw the pressing equipment, the mini-haberdashery, and the lack of personal space for Brown's star running back. He arranged for Pollard to have a separate room for his living quarters and up-to-date pressing equipment. Rockefeller covered all the costs. At least for a time Pollard was into a business that well suited him.

JOHN D. ROCKEFELLER, JR.

Years later and again to improve his financial situation Pollard went into the coal business in 1933 in New York City. That's right, the black combustible fossil fuel stuff from Pennsylvania and West Virginia you burn to heat the furnace during cold spells was his way to deal with the Great Depression. He borrowed money to get started. He hired a small fleet of trucks to carry the coal from the wholesalers to his customers in Harlem. Each truck featured his name in large, bold print. At that time his name still had recognition in the Black community given his exploits on the gridiron. The business did well enough to provide a living. He was able to rent office space in the General Motors Building on Fifth Avenue and to move into the Washington Heights area of Harlem. This was at a time when Harlem was still considered the "Negro Mecca," a place where Black artists, musicians, and writers flourished. Thanks to dead plant matter decaying into peat, which in turn was converted into coal by the heat and pressure over the eons, Pollard had found another way to make an honest buck.

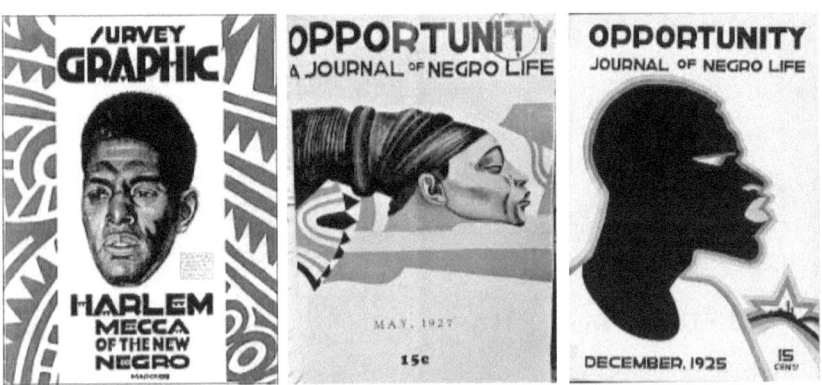

In 1935 Pollard got into another venture. He founded a weekly newspaper, *The New York Independent News.* It was a risky decision to be in competition with the white newspapers, which were widely read by educated Blacks. Two other papers had tried to compete. *The New York News* had floundered financially and gone out of business. *The New York Amsterdam News* was tied down in a bitter labor dispute and about to go under. Pollard was betting he could make a go of it.

As might be expected the paper gave extensive coverage to Black athletes and entertainers. His stories featured stories about Joe Louis. The "Bronx Bomber" was the heavyweight-boxing champion of the world. The paper also covered and Negro baseball teams, including the New York Black Yankees, who were in business from 1931 to 1948. Their home games were played in Yankee Stadium with relatively good attendance.

When they played against white players they were always competitive.

THE OTHER YANKEE TEAM

Pollard had his own column in the paper. His by-line was *Sports by Fritz*. He praised Black athletes and continuously argued for the integration of professional baseball and football. He pointed out a fascinating connection between sports and entertainers in other fields. Not only did Black athletes have to play at the highest possible standards, they also had to entertain with flashy moves in order to stand out from the crowd. Pollard's paper was progressive on social issues and conservative concerning fiscal matters. The editorial page was staunchly opposed to racial discrimination and always a supporter of integration in the marketplace, home purchases, the public schools, and all public accommodations. As an example...When New York City held the 1939 World's Fair Pollard strenuously pushed the city to hire Blacks and to include reasonable exhibition space for Black-Americans.

ENTRY INTO THE WORLD'S FAIR

Blacks certainly needed Pollard's advocacy. According to many the New York Fair Corporation restricted job opportunities for Blacks. The Black press decried the placing of Blacks only in the capacities of maids and porters. It was argued that Blacks were only given menial parts in the great fair, which was to showcase "the truly democratic world of tomorrow." The New York World's Fair Corporation denied any bias in hiring practices. Be that as it may, two Black contributions stand out.

The acclaimed Harlem sculptor, Augusta Savage, was commissioned to create a work for the fair. Her sculpture was called *The Harp.* It was displayed in the Contemporary Arts Building. The work was inspired by the song *Lift Every Voice and Sing.* It was written by James Weldon Johnson to celebrate the birthday of Abraham Lincoln. The song was first sung by school children in Jacksonville, Florida.

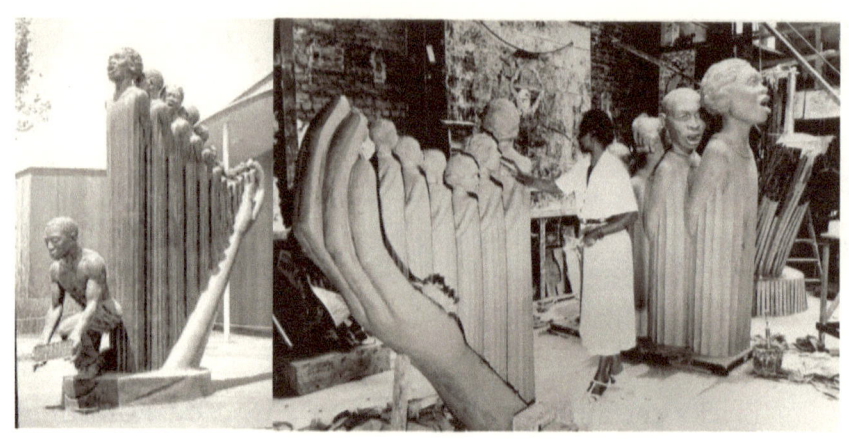

THE HARP

The sculpture depicted a group of twelve stylized Black singers. They were posed in graduated heights. They symbolized the strings of the harp. The sounding board of the harp was formed by the hand and arm of God. A kneeling man held music that represented the foot pedal. Apparently, no funds were available to cast *The Harp* or facilities to store it. When the Fair closed Savage's work was demolished as were all the art in the Contemporary Arts Building. What a shame. What has lasted, however, are the beautiful, inspiring lyrics of James Weldon Johnson. His words are sometimes referred to as the Black National Anthem.

JAMES W. JOHNSON

Lift every voice and sing
Till earth and heaven ring,
Ring with the harmonies of Liberty, Let
our rejoicing rise
High as the listening skies,
Let it resound loud as the rolling sea.
Sing a song full of the faith that the dark past has taught us,
Sing a song full of the hope that the present has brought
us,

Facing the rising sun of our new day begun. Let
us march on till victory is won.

The lyrics reminded Blacks that each generation has to lift its voice and demand protection of their human rights. Certainly this was the credo of Fritz Pollard as he sought social justice.

God of our weary years
God of our silent tears,
Thou who has brought us thus far on the way;
Thou who has by Thy might
Lead us into the light,
Keep us forever in the path, we pray.

Some Blacks were employed as entertainers. Unfortunately, these roles were often built on racial stereotypes commonly held by the white community. By way of example, Bill "Bojangles" Robinson performed in *Hot Mikado*. This was a jazz version of Gilbert and Sullivan's operetta. It was one of the biggest hits in the 1936 World's Fair.

Another example was Frank Buck's Jungle Land. Black men wore costumes depicting them as native Africans. Multiple stereotypes found their way into this exhibit, while reinforcing latent Jim Crow attitudes.

To its credit the World's Fair Corporation did provide a major opportunity for Blacks to visit the Fair. Of course, not all Blacks could afford the tab in the lingering days of the Great Recession. It cost 50-cents for an adult and 25-cents for children to enter the Fair. The average family spent $20.00. That would be about $340 in today's currency. This was at a time when the average hourly wage was 66-cents and the average weekly salary was about $20.30. For many Blacks that was a lot.

Pollard's newspaper career showed at least two things: first, a Black owned and run newspaper could be successful, both in circulation and revenue. Second, coverage of the Black community was important and useful in pushing back against discrimination and advocating for integration. Between 1935 and 1942 the weekly circulation of 35,000 proved these points. In this vein he supported the view that "you need not buy where they won't hire you." That was Black Pride long before the term was coined. Who would have thought this of a football player?

THE THIRD QUARTER

Football is an honest game. It's true to life. It's a game about sharing. Football is a team game. So is life.

Joe Namath, Quarterback

The tide of battle began to turn in the muddy slug match in Tournament Park. At the beginning of the third quarter Coach Dietz inserted Ralph Boone. He was a big, pow-erful kid with bulging biceps who took over the halfback position for Washington State. The Cougars would now attack the edges of the Brown defense once they got the ball. By the end of the game Boone would carry the ball three out of every five plays. Overall the WSC would gain 202-yards on the ground in the second half. Brown would barely run for 17-yards.

Brown kicked off to start the third quarter. Using repeated line plunges the team from Pullman moved the ball deep into Brown territory only to lose it when Benton "Bill" Bangs fumbled. Unable to move the ball the Bears had to punt. Relentlessly the Cougars moved the ball up and down the field until Boone barreled into the end zone on a three-yard rush. The scoreless tie was broken. Beyond the issue of cleats the key to Washington State's success was a new formation Dietz employed. Two sturdy linemen shifted over from the left to the right side, and the backs formed a V-shape behind them. Boone would start toward his right tackle and then veer inside or outside depending on the blocking. The Cougars seemed to knock the Brown defensive line back three feet on every play. As for Pollard's team they simply couldn't move the ball. It was the cleat issue again. Toward the end of the third quarter Coach Robinson yanked the entire backfield. It didn't help. The backups proved equally unable to move the ball. The original backfield was restored at the beginning of the last quarter.

POLLARD TRIES TO BREAK THE TIE

One can only imagine what a dejected Fritz Pollard was thinking in the waning moments of the third quarter. Since the closest thing to God is a football coach the run-ning back had no choice but to sit on the bench. Weary, cloaked in mud, and unable to run against the underrated

Washington State defense, this was not the game he imag-ined on the long train ride to Pasadena. He was learning how humbling the game might be for even a great player. On the other hand he had no idea what the next football season would bring, or the years that would follow.

The 1916 football season was a banner year for Eastern college teams. The final rankings for the top five teams were:

Army   8 – 0
Pittsburgh 8 – 0
Brown   8 – 1
Colgate   8 – 1
Yale   8 – 1

On November 11, 1916 Fritz Pollard's Brown Bears played a return game with Yale in New Haven. Once again the Yale Bowl hosted the game. Over 25,000 fans attended the game. The Yale Team was loaded and undefeated.

Yale 25   Carnegie Tech 0
Yale 61   Virginia 3
Yale 12   Lehigh 0
Yale 19   VIP 0
Yale 36   Washington and Jefferson 14
Yale 7   Colgate 3

The Brown team seemed equally powerful.

Brown 18   Rhode Island State 0
Brown 42   Trinity 0
Brown 69   Amherst 0
Brown 20   Williams 0
Brown 21   Rutgers 3
Brown 42   Vermont 0

Edward N. Robinson was in his 15th season as the head coach at Brown. Yale was coached by Tad Jones. He was in his first year. The vet and the youth were about to square off and for the first time players wore numerals on their jerseys. As in the previous game in 1915 Fritz Pollard was again pelted with racial insults as he took the field. Once again the Yale fans sang *Bye, Bye Black Bird*. Pollard would later refer to the incident as being "Nig--rized." As always he was determined to let his play speak for itself. He held his tongue and fists. He couldn't make an issue of racism. Rather, he would return punts at full speed. He hurdled tacklers and eluded others with his quickness and blinding speed. He again proved to be an able blocker and an excellent tackler. Though small for the game he was a sound, fundamental player.

The first half was difficult for Brown. Yale kept the pigskin in Brown territory most of the first half. The Brown team was forced to make a goal line stand. Another threat was stopped by Pollard by way of an interception. At halftime Yale led 6-0 thanks to two field goals. The first half statistics were not appealing. Brown had run only 25-offensive plays for a total of forty yards gained. Pollard carried the ball three times for 28-yards. This was not something to write home about.

The second half was different. Using a series of short rushes, Brown moved the ball downfield. Then came the big run. Pollard took the ball on the 39-yard line, bolted outside and weaved his way down field to the Yale 5-yard line. The Yale line stiffened and held but the tide was slowly turning. Pollard was heating up. With the ball again Pollard made a spectacular catch and raced to the Yale 3-yrd line. A play later Pollard scored. The period ended with Brown ahead 7 to 6.

The final quarter began with a booming Yale punt that Pollard retrieved on the Brown 40-yard line. *The New York Times* reported what then took place.

Pollard dexterously threw off the Yale ends, started toward the right, drawing the entire pack of the Yale tacklers in that direction, then using a puzzling side step, switched to the left where he outstripped every Yale pursuer in a desperate spring for the Yale goal line, sailing across with the second touchdown for the visitors.

Pollard's run broke the back of the Yale team. The New Haven boys never threatened after that play. The Yale coach was quoted after the game.

Please don't mention Pollard. I can still see him racing across the goal line. I wouldn't be surprised if he wasn't just about the best ball carrier any of us ever saw.

The New York Age addressed Pollard's success as "doing a great deal to help solve the race problem. That was the general opinion of the Black press. Pollard was now symbolizing something more than just his heroics on the football field.

1916 BROWN FOOTBALL TEAM

Yale finished its season with two victories, 10-0 over Princeton and 6-3 over Harvard. Brown played Harvard the next week and won 21-0. The last game of the season would be against Colgate sporting an excellent team with a record of 6-1 coming into the game. The Red Raiders had a chip on their shoulders.

Colgate 34   Susquehanna 0
Colgate 28   Maine 0
Colgate 25   Illinois 3
Colgate 33   Rhode Island 0
Colgate 27   Springfield 14
Colgate 3   Yale 7
Colgate 15   Syracuse 0

After losing to Yale the team dedicated its season to beating Brown. To this end the team arrived outside of Providence one week before the game and practiced endlessly the strategy used to beat Syracuse: line plunges. This proved fortuitous since the weather turned bad and the skies opened up. It was the 1916 Rose Bowl all over: a mud splattered field. Trying to help their team the Brown students scattered hay all over Andrews Field. They wanted to protect the field from frost. Their efforts, though well intended, were drenched by a heavy rainfall. At 11:30 a.m. on Thanksgiving Day the teams lined up on a soggy, hay strewn field before a crowd estimated at nine thousand shivering fans.

There was a lot at stake in the Colgate-Brown game. If Brown won the team had a shot at being awarded the mythical national championship. A loss would let Army or Pitt, both undefeated, with a chance for the title. A victory by Brown could lead to Fritz Pollard being named an All-American if he had a great game.

The Colgate team proved too powerful, scoring in each quarter and winning 28 – 0. Brown was solidly beaten. In defeat Pollard was recognized for his great play, especially on defense. *The New York Times* applauded him, saying Colgate "could not get him out of the way." The paper pointed out that Pollard was the "one man on the Brown team who was able to tumble the overwhelming Colgate rush." Though Colgate players successfully shook off Brown tacklers the one person they couldn't elude was Pollard. He always seemed to be outguessing the opposition. In the end, however, Colgate was the superior team. The loss ended Brown's hope of being the mythical national champion.

There's no question that Fritz Pollard wanted to be designated an All-American. Such a tribute marked you as an elite football player. When the *New York Times* named him to its All-Eastern football team in December that was a good start. In doing so the paper described the Brown running back as "easily the greatest half back of the year." Though this merit was well deserved and special the real question concerned the mythical All-American team selected by Walter Camp, who was considered the dean of American football coaches and for some the "father of American football." He was inducted into the College Football Hall of Fame as a coach in 1951.

Camp played football at Yale, later coached at the university, and eventually participated on many collegiate football rules committees. Among the changes he helped bring to football:

- a line of scrimmage.
- the snap-back from the center.
- a system of downs.
- a 7 man line.
- a 4 man backfield - quarterback, fullback, 2 halfbacks
- a safety of 2 points
- lower the number of players from 15 to 11
- add measuring lines on the field

WALTER CAMP AT YALE

Fortunately for Pollard, Walter Camp saw Pollard during his last three games of the season. What he witnessed caused him to place Pollard on the first team of All-Americans. In describing Pollard he said the Brown runner was "the most elusive back of the year or of any year." Camp pointed out that anyone who saw the Colgate game realized what a great defensive back he was as he stopped the opposition again and again with sure tackles. Curiously, Pollard heard the news while he was delivering cleaned and pressed clothes around the campus. *The Chicago Herald* of the white press commented: Pollard has proven "that color is not an insuperable handicap to honor on the field of sport." It should be noted that Fritz Pollard was the second Black to be recognized by Walter Camp. The first was William H. Lewis.

LEWIS OF HARVARD

Lewis was born in Berkley, Virginia in 1868. He was the son of a former slave. He attended Amherst College in Massachusetts, where he was one of the first Black football players. He went on to Harvard Law School. There he continued to play the rough and tumble game. He achieved at the highest levels, both in his academic pursuits and on the field. He was the first Black in the sport to be selected an All-American in 1900 for his play at center. During his long and productive life as an attorney he was an inspirational voice to end the disenfranchisement of Blacks. In 1902 he stated his case. He spoke before the Amherst College alumni, stating that race was the "transcendent problem facing the country." He then talked about the recent Spanish-American War.

Yesterday the United States waged a war for humanity where tyranny and oppression had grown intolerable. Only a few hundreds of miles south of us are 10,000,000 people who are deprived of their rights, who are practically in a state of serfdom. Thousands have been lynched and shot for attempting to exercise the God given rights of every human being. The great Democratic Party rolls on its honied tongue the sweet morsels of 'consent of the governed' and 'equality of man.' The Republican Party, progressive, patriotic, absorbed with expansion is too busy to disturb the harmony of the spheres. They stand opposite making grimaces at each other; one says 'Filipino' the other hasn't the courage to say 'Nig--r.' It is a beautiful game of football with the Negro as the football.

One can assume that Fritz Pollard felt like the football in question, disciplined and toughened by the game, proving on the field that he was the equal of any man, yet never fully accepted by some because of the color of his skin. Still, he lived in the present and sought a future less harsh and fairer. In this he was a brother to Lewis. Speaking before the Tuskegee Normal and Industrial Institution class in 1910 in Alabama, Lewis said:

Love your native Southland. Nine tenths of our people were born here. All of our past is here. All our future is here. Here most of us will live and here pass to the great majority and be gathered to the ashes of our fathers. The most glorious history of our race is here in the Southland, the most glorious history of the negro race anywhere in the world is here. If we have suffered here, we have also achieved here. Rejoice in everything that is Southern.

What was Lewis getting at? Succinctly, as with Pollard, America was home to Blacks and a potential future beyond the heritage of slavery, Jim Crow, and "separate but equal." That future was bright and distant but possible.

––––––––––

The 1916 season was over and Fritz Pollard had made his mark. He would soon enter Dartmouth College to study to be a dentist. The future looked bright. What could possibly go wrong?

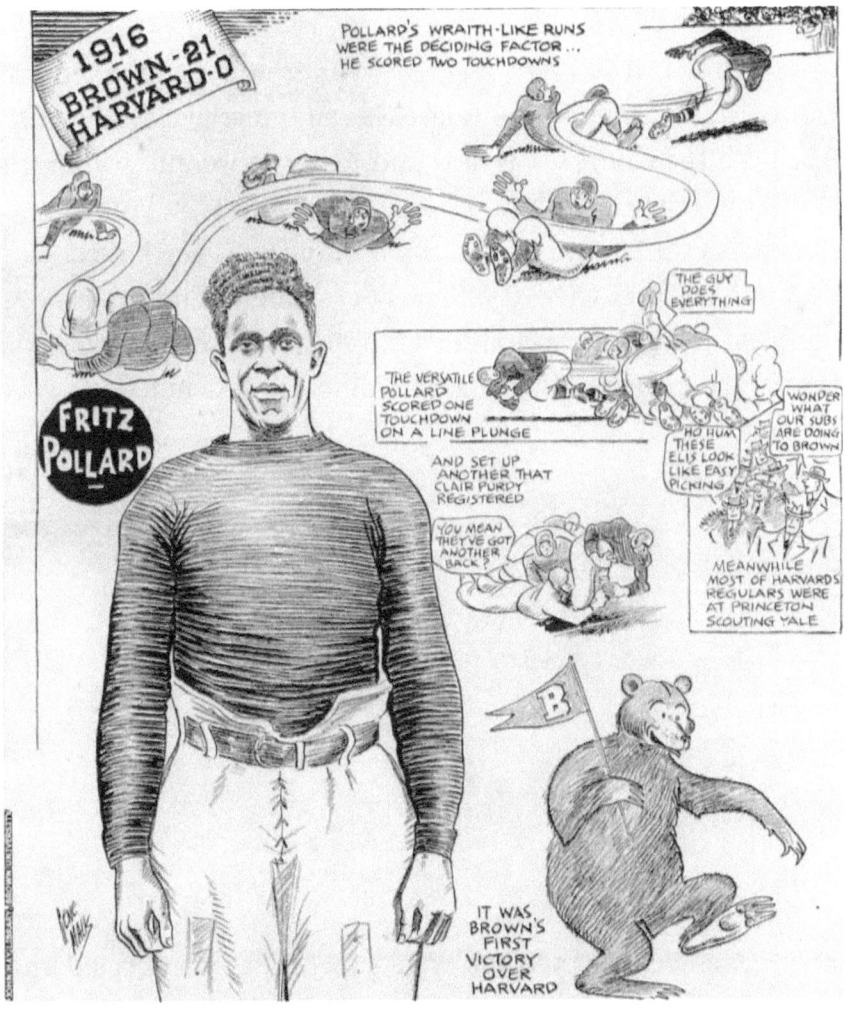

CHAPTER 11 – WAR

On April 2, 1917 President Woodrow Wilson asked the United States Congress to declare war on Imperial Germany. On April 6th the Congress agreed and America went to war as an ally of the Triple Entente composed of Great Britain, France, and Russia. As the country geared up for conflict a track meet was held in New York City. The Smart Set Athletic Club sponsored the event. The Club was founded in 1904 and assembled the first formal independent Black basketball team. It debuted in 1907.

BLACK BASKETBALL

Members of the Club were generally well educated and affluent. They lived in a mainly white neighborhood called Stuyvesant Heights in Brooklyn. The track meet was held over two days, April 16 and 17, 1917 in the Regiment Armory in Brooklyn. Fritz Pollard was entered in the 65-yard low hurdles. In winning the event he beat two premier runners including the reigning national champion. He ran the track in 8-seconds, which was flying in those days.

RUNNING FOR BROWN

Things were looking good for Pollard. He was a sparkling runner on the gridiron. He was a flash on the track. He was considering dentistry school at Dartmouth and doing a little coaching in addition to his pressing business. Wilson's war resolution, however, threw a monkey wrench into his immediate future. The country was moving into a fighting mode. Young men were being conscripted into the armed forces, including Blacks. Understandably this created a dilemma for them. Wilson wanted to make "the world safe for democracy" at a time when Jim Crow laws defined Blacks as second-class citizens and when race riots and Black men were too often lynched. Some Black voices pointed out the obvious. Making the world safe didn't always include Georgia, Mississippi, or Alabama, nor did it make life easier in the North where discrimination based on racial attitudes existed. On the other hand Blacks were being drafted. Eventually over 370,000 Blacks would serve in the armed forces. There was a need to support the country and to hope for fairness and opportunity in the military. All this impacted Pollard, as well as two personal issues. His brother Hughes was fighting with the French on the Western Front. In this sense the Pollard family was already at war. Since Fritz Pollard was married and supporting a family, he was not in danger of being drafted. Unless he volunteered he could continue on as a civilian. Pollard had to find a middle ground.

A DICHOTOMY OF FEELINGS

In February 1918, Pollard dropped out of school and entered military service. He was offered and accepted a position as a physical director of the Army's Young Men's Christian Association (YMCA). He would be stationed at Fort Meade in Maryland. He was part of the Army's efforts to place known college athletes as physical directors of the YMCA's classes in many camps. The Army's motivation was two-fold: first, get the guys in shape; second, attempt to quiet the racial tensions overtaking the country even as he prepared to fight the Hun. The Army didn't need racial problems in the camps. What was going on was a reflection of a wider situation in the country. There was a massive migration of Southern blacks to the North for better jobs, housing, and education, and to get away from the overt violence of the South. The issue of race always hovered in the background, sometimes inert, at other times explosive, but always a threat.

At Camp Mead Pollard served alongside a hundred commissioned Black officers. They had been trained in separate facilities when the Army was rife with racial attitudes. As such Black officers were seldom treated with respect. They were never put in charge of white draftees. Moreover, they were not permitted to rise above the rank of captain. They would be washed out for incompetence whenever possible. In this environment Pollard went to work. As always he seemed to get along with everyone. Perhaps growing up in a white community helped, at least that's what he always maintained. Or was it his status as a football player? He wasn't just another guy. He was an elite athlete. In any event he had learned the lessons of Jack Johnson and what his older brothers taught him about surviving in a white world. Beyond that he was proud of his service.

IN THE MILITARY

Later in the year he was reassigned to a new position. The War Department had a new Student Army Training Corps program (SATC). Pollard would be the director of one of the college sites. He was assigned to an SATC group at Lincoln University, a small historically Black school located in Oxford, Pennsylvania, approximately 40-miles from Philadelphia. The college was established in 1854, only a handful of years before the firing on Fort Sumter in Charleston harbor. John Miller Dickey is credited with founding the school. He was a white Presbyterian minister. It was originally called the Ashman Institute and was established to provide higher education for capable Black students from around the country, who were unable to attend other schools because of prevailing racial attitudes. The school was renamed Lincoln University following the assassination of President Abraham. The college was noted for its progressive curriculum. It did not focus primarily on vocational and technical skills. It emphasized the liberal arts and provided an education for future doctors and lawyers.

JOHN MILLER DICKEY

For over a hundred years (1854 – 1954) graduates of Lincoln University made up 20% of Black physicians in the country and over 10% of Black lawyers. The school's alumni include Thurgood Marshall (Justice of the Supreme Court), Langton Hughes (poet), Cab Calloway (musician), and Paul Robeson (singer and attorney) among others.

THURGOOD MARSHALL   CAB CALLOWAY

When Fritz Pollard was stationed at Lincoln University there were only 140 students on campus. Today there are about 2,000 students on campus. He had a most busy schedule. After taking his Dental School classes at the University of Pennsylvania and attending to his family in Philadelphia, Pollard took a noon train to Oxford, where he wore two caps. He met his duties as the athletic director as prescribed by the Army. In addition he was the head football coach of the school's team, the Lincoln Lions. He was credited with bringing an innovative double-wing formation and a wide-open style of play he had first learned at Brown. He, as would be expected, emphasized solid defense and even scrimmaged with his players. For all this he was paid $50 a month. Interestingly Leslie Pollard had attended Lincoln where he coached the team in 1914. Recall he was Fritz Pollard's older brother and mentor.

LESLIE POLLARD (STANDING, FAR LEFT)

The big game of the year was always the Lincoln-Howard game, sometimes referred to as "the Classic." On Thanksgiving Day Pollard's team defeated Howard 13 – 0 in a memorable 1918 game. His Lincoln players finished the season undefeated. He had his first taste of coaching. It would not be his last.

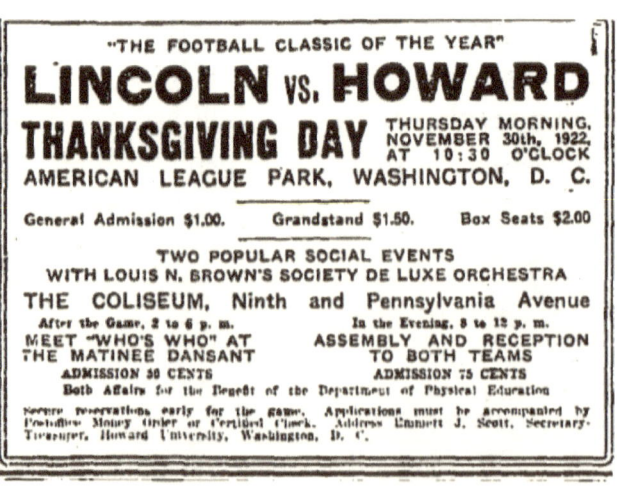

Beyond the heroics on the football field the reality of the war lingered in Black consciousness.

REMEMBERING WHAT THEY FOUGHT FOR

CHAPTER 12 – GOING PRO

A week before Lincoln University played Virginia Union in 1919 Fritz Pollard received an overture from Ralph "Fat" Waldsmith. He was the owner and coach of the Akron Pros, a professional football team. The Akron team needed new players to juice up the team against its chief rivals, Massillon and Canton, both strong teams in Ohio. An improved team and record might translate into increased gate revenues. Pollard decided to play. No contract was involved. It was to be a one game deal or at most a few games still remaining on the Akron schedule. On Saturday Pollard coached his Lincoln team to a 12 – 6 victory and then took two trains to reach Akron. He arrived in the city Sunday morning, the day of the game. Apparently he had trouble getting to the game. No white cabbie would stop for him. Eventually one did. He was aware of Pollard's football heroics and welcomed him to the town. This was not completely true of his teammates. Many were from the South and saw Pollard as just another "nig--r," even though playing days at Brown preceded him. As fate would have it the quarterback on the Akron team was Chair Purdy. He had played with Pollard at Brown. He helped to relieve racial tensions.

The Akron team was part of the American Professional Football Association. Its inaugural season was 1920. An agreement was signed on August 20, 1920. The first four teams were based in Ohio and were sometimes referred to as "the Ohio League." The charter members included:

. Akron Pros
. Cleveland Tigers

. Canton Bulldogs
. Dayton Triangles

A second meeting was held later in the year. Other teams were offered an opportunity to join the new league. Eight additional teams joined to include the states of Illinois and Michigan. The first president of the league was the renowned Jim Thorpe, the great player from Carlisle Indian School in Pennsylvania. He was also a member of the Canton Bulldogs. The APFA would be renamed the National Football League (NFL) in 1920. At that time Fritz Pollard would be playing for Akron and co-coaching. This would make him the first Black coach in the NFL in both capacities.

The game against Massillon began with death threats against Pollard as reported in the *Akron Beacon Journal*. It was suggested that members of the Massillon team were going to harm Pollard. Neither of this occurred. The opposition did pile on Pollard but nothing more. As always he came up smiling. Massillon won the game 13 – 6 before a crowd of 8,500 fans at Goodrich Field. Pollard distinguished himself by scoring the only Akron touchdown and, of course, with his defensive play and sensational punt returns. He received $200 for the game and expenses. This game marked the start of Pollard's 8-year career in professional football.

Only six blacks were in the APFA either before Pollard or as a contemporary. They included:

- Charles W. Follis (1902 – 1906) – The Shelby Athletic Club. He is generally considered the first Black player in professional football. One of his teammates was the legendary Branch Rickey who would one day sign Jackie Robinson to a professional baseball contract with the Brooklyn Dodgers.

- Charles Young (1906 – 1908, 1911) Akron Pros

- Henry McDonald (1911 – 1917) Rochester Jeffersons

- Gordon "Charlie" Smith (1915) Canton Bulldogs

- Robert "Rube" Marshall (1919-1920) Rock Island Independents

These early players laid the groundwork for the stars of today in the NFL. We should not forget their contribution to an integrated professional football league.

CHARLES YOUNG   HENRY MCDONALD

Who was the first Black player in the NFL? Fritz Pollard is usually given the nod, but there is some controversy to that designation. Both Pollard and Robert Marshall began their pro careers in 1919, one year before the birth of the NFL. Both Akron and Rock Island were charter members of the NFL,

Marshall and Pollard should share the honor. However, the Rock Island team played its first game one-week before Pollard took to the field. Technically, Marshall was the first if you accept that argument.

ROBERT MARSHALL   POLLARD AND MARSHALL (CENTER)

The 1920 season was one to be remembered. Professional football was changing. Efforts were being made to clean up the sport by stopping:

. betting on the games.
. thrown games.
. dirty play.
. poor officiating.
. players jumping from one team to another.
. hiring of collegians.

It was also Fritz Pollard's first full season in professional football and he was a marked man. Fans came to see him either to be hurt or to be wildly successful. He had to dress outside of the stadium. He was then driven to the game at the last possible moment. He then sprinted onto the field a few minutes before the kickoff. Once the game started he was a constant target of rough play, even efforts meant to hurt him. He was called foul names by fans and players alike. Most restaurants and hotels did not want to see him at first. He was off limits. However, as the season progressed and Akron's success mounted on the field, there was a change of heart. Pollard was now a celebrity and that was good for business. All this took place during a championship year. The 1920 record attests to that:

Akron 43 – 0 over the Wheeling Stogies
Akron 37 – 0 over the Columbus Panhandles
Akron 13 – 0 over the Cincinnati Celts
Akron 7 – 0 over the Massillon Tigers
Akron 10 – 0 over the Canton Bulldogs
Akron 7 – 7 tie with the Detroit Heralds
Akron 13 – 0 over the Dayton Triangles
Akron 7 – 0 over the Canton Bulldogs
Akron 0 – 0 tie with the Buffalo All-Americans

Akron was undefeated and had the best record. It was also an integrated team. They were claimed the APFA champion.

WORLDS CHAMPS
Akron — 1920 — Professionals

TOP ROW: Read left to right: Mgr. Art Ranny, Nash, Benny Leonard, Nesser, Bailey, Capt. Copley, Crawford, Cobb, Bierce, King, Asst Mgr.
BOTTOM ROW — Johnson, McCormack, Harris, Tomlin, Sweetland, Garret, Pollard.

CHAPTER 13 – FIGHTING BACK

Fritz Pollard had a problem. His professional football career was over. No longer would he dazzle fans with long runs on the turf as he eluded the lunges of strong-armed tacklers on his way to the end zone. His coaching days were also over or at least it seemed that way. Other lines of work had attracted him, including being a talent scout and agent, especially for Black artists. He had also delved into the tax consulting business quite by accident and had done quite well helping well-heeled clients who were dealing with the IRS. With his business acumen he had established an investment business that catered to the Black community to increase their knowledge and ability to purchase stocks and bonds. By 1929 he was doing quite well and then came Black Friday and the seeds of the Great Depression were planted. As was the case of millions of others he had to struggle to keep his head above the drenching waters of unemployment and emotional turbulence. This he did. Still he had a problem and it had nothing to do with the economic calamity befalling the country, at least not outwardly.

Pollard was engaged in a quiet war with something that didn't exist on paper or in any public record, yet had tangible consequences especially on Sunday afternoons in the fall. The struggle would last over a decade, between 1933 and 1946, a period when no Black football players were in the NFL due to a Gentlemen's Agreement to keep the game lily white. Pollard wanted to end the non-existent ban. He couldn't take it on directly. To hopefully integrate professional football he would need an end run to end the institutional racism of his day. It came in the form of Herschel "Rip" Day, a Black athletic promoter in Harlem who had attended Lincoln University. He was putting together a Black football team as a counterweight to the NFL and he needed a coach.

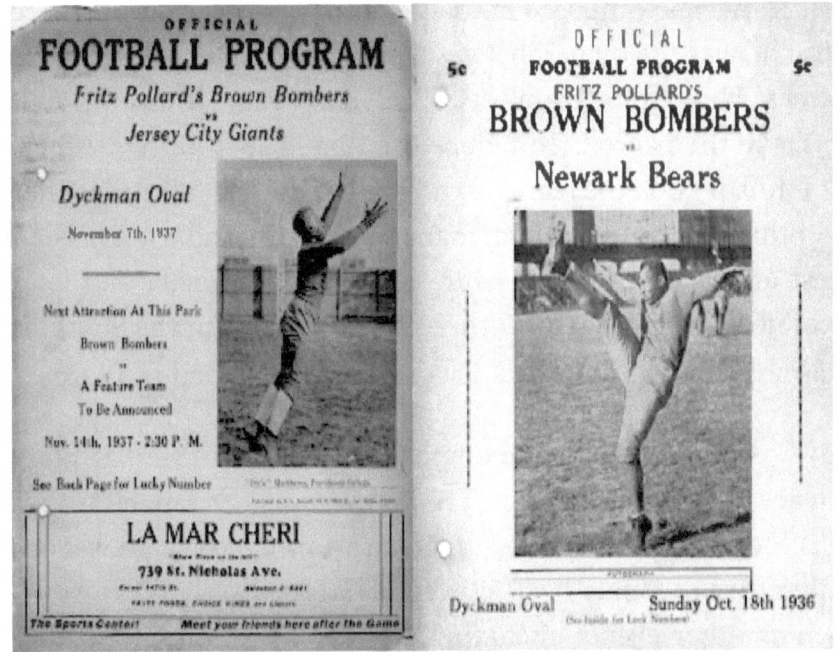

THE BROWN BOMBERS

Day found his coach in Fritz Pollard. He would be in charge of the Brown Bombers, who were so named to honor Joe Louis, an aspiring heavyweight. Of course, Pollard was a natural choice. He had played football at Brown. He had coached at Lincoln University. He had played and coached with the Akron Pros. Though talented and experienced there was another reason why he was the right man for the job. He had done this before with another team.

In 1928, Pollard had formed an all-star professional football team on the South Side of Chicago. The team would include Black all-stars. Even then he wanted to prove that an integrated team could play ball without ugly incidents. The team was called the Chicago Black Hawks and they played football, not hockey. Games were scheduled against white professional teams and semi-pro teams in the Chicago area. The team was composed of rookies and vets. Pollard wore three hats: he was the owner; he was the coach; and he played in the games. Though the team was talented as always it was difficult to make the payroll. To reduce the financial strain Dr. Albert C. Johnson took the team on the road in the late fall and winter months. He was the general manager. The touring team headed west and played against white teams in California and later exhibition games against other all Black teams in the South. It was not enough. The Black Hawks were disbanded in 1932.

Creating the Brown Bomber team was one thing. Finding a place to play was another. The answer was Dyckman Oval. It was located at the northern end of Manhattan in New York City. It was a venue hosting Negro League baseball games, as well as other events, including boxing, wrestling, ice-skating competitions, and football games. The Oval could host between 4,500 to 10,000 fans. Those attending the game had easy access to the venue since the Dyckman train station provided a stop close to the park.

What Day and Pollard wanted to do was showcase Black collegiate talent to counter the argument that Blacks couldn't compete with NFL players. They also wanted to prove that integrated teams could play the game without rancor. Together they wanted to schedule games against NFL teams. Head to head competition would prove the obvious. There was Black football talent available. The NFL owners refused to schedule games with the Brown Bombers. They were not interested in disrupting their racist business model. Because of the depression and the high unemployment ranks, they didn't want to be seen giving limited job openings to Blacks at the expense of whites. They, as the argument went, wanted to keep their white fan base intact. In today's vernacular it was institutional racism, discriminatory and obscene. Unfairly, the ban cheated all fans of the hidden talent sitting on the bench. Given that, the Brown Bombers were forced to schedule games against local teams.

BROWN BOMBERS 1935

No.	Name	Position	Weight	School
12	Benny Brown	Tackle	230	Howard University
14	Livingston	Tackle	225	Wiley
22	Holder	Tackle	230	Iowa
21	Conrad	Back	238	Morgan
20	Sparkman	Center	210	W. Va. State
8	Early	Tackle	227	U. S. Navy
15	Smith	Guard	220	U. of Indiana
13	Rogers	End	180	New Haven
5	Williams	Guard	195	Morgan
19	Lilliard	Quarterback	192	Oregon
4	Summers	Back	170	Morehouse
7	Reynolds	Guard	195	Augusta College
10	Gill	Back	170	Santa Clara Teachers
17	Carter	Guard	200	Ala. State Teachers
6	Dave Meyers	Back	200	N. Y. U.
11	Leonard	End	200	Mich. State
9	Bergen	End	180	Lincoln
8	Dial	Back	175	Santa Clara Teachers
16	Alston	Back	201	Ken. State
2	Wallace	End	185	Union University
3	Hansborough	Back	175	N. Y. U.
1	Lee	End	190	Howard

Pollard was motivated to integrate the NFL. It was as simple as that.

I did everything I could to open the doors and make it easier for them (Black players). When I organized the Brown Bomber team, and there weren't any Black boys in the pro leagues, I did that deliberately to show them that they could play against a whole Black team and not have any trouble or any prejudice, and could draw a good crowd.

Unfortunately, regardless of his efforts the NFL didn't buckle. The ban remained in effect. The case of Ozzie Simmons proved that point. Even the most successful and skilled Black players would never get a contract. Even a player who could help an NFL team win a championship was deemed unacceptable.

Oze E. "Ozzie" Simmons was raised in Gainesville, Texas and was a standout quarterback in a segregated high school in Fort Worth. An Iowa alumnus saw Simmons play. He recommended his school and Simmons gave it a try. Iowa was a good call. The university had Blacks on the football team since 1895. Unannounced Simmons showed up in Iowa City to the surprise of the Iowa coaches. As the story goes they gave the kid a chance to show his stuff in practice. He did so, returning two punts for touchdowns. The coaches then told Simmons, "We'll find you a place to stay." During his career at Iowa (1934-1936) Simmons lettered and set many Iowa records besides being named an All-American. It was not enough. The NFL did not bend. No team offered him a contract.

OZE E. "OZZIE" SIMMONS

Since Simmons was the only Black player on the Hawkeye team he was the target of opposing players, which led to many injuries. This was especially true if the other team had no Black players. This was the case against the University of Minnesota. Twelve years earlier in 1922 Jack Trice was killed by injuries sustained in a game against the Golden Gophers. In 1934 Simmons was knocked out of the game three times with injuries. He was unable to play in the second half leading to a lop-sided Minnesota victory. The game was blatantly racist.

Opposing players piled on Simmons. Many kneed him. The refs did not call obvious penalties. In Des Moines the radio announcer for the game was Ronald Reagan. He pointed out:

The problems were when you played another team that did not have a Black. For some reason or another, then they would pick on this one man.

Continuing the future President of the United States recounted a game against Illinois when Simmons was injured twice and his team stood up for him.

I saw (Iowa players) Dick Crayne and Ted Osmaloski walk over to the Illinois huddle during a timeout, and after the game I found out what they said: "Do that to Simmons once more, and we're going to run you right out of the end of your stadium."

PRESIDENT REAGAN

When the teams met the next year the Governor of Iowa warned the Minnesota coaching staff, stating: "If the officials stand for any rough tactics like Minnesota used last year, I'm sure the crowd won't." Extra security was called for the game. Though tensions ran high there was no trouble. Again Iowa lost the game, this time in a fair fight.

It was difficult for the Brown Bombers to make a go of it financially. Part of the problem was the scant media coverage of the day. The white press seldom covered the Brown Bombers unless they were playing a white team. The Black press delivered the news on Thursdays, providing modest coverage of the previous Sunday games. Since the fans already knew the score this was old news. This being the case attendance was always a problem. Revenue never exceeded expense, though Pollard tried many "stunts" to attract more fans. For example: the players sang spirituals as they came to the line of scrimmage. Unorthodox formations were used to spice up the game and hopefully to mystify the opposition. All this helped but not enough. In time the game clock ran out for the Brown Bombers and Fritz Pollard had failed to end the NFL's exclusionary policy, and at that moment he had not heard of a kid who would later star at UCLA. His name was Kenny Washington.

KENNY WASHINGTON

THE FOURTH QUARTER

Leadership is a matter of having people look at you and gain confidence. If you're in control, they're in control.

Tom Landry, Football Coach

Late in the third quarter the Washington State team started an 80-yard march down the field. At the beginning of the fourth quarter this drive culminated in a Cougar touchdown. Carl Dietz, the Washington fullback put his head down and plowed through the mud to a TD. Carl Dietz was not related to the Washington State coach. The score was now 14 – 0. The rest of the final quarter show-cased relentless futility for both teams as the muddy con-ditions hindered play. The second Rose Bowl was history. For Fritz Pollard and the Brown team the game statistic told all.

Team Stats	WSC	Brown
First Downs	19	6
Rushing Yards	313	74
Passing Yards	0	12
Total Yards	313	86
Fumbles	2	6
Punt Average	7-37	13-29

Pollard racked up 47 yards in 13 carries wearing the wrong cleats. Wearing the right cleats Carl Dietz car-ried 33 times for 105 yards. He was deservingly named the MVP. As for Pollard...The LA Times said this about his play:

The gentleman of color and his ability hardly per-formed up to his advance notice. Speed is one of his great-est assets, but the slippery field made it of little use to him. He made some gains but could never break away for long runs. Once or twice, he was trapped behind his own line before he could get up stream and could do nothing but dodge back and forth. He was slippery as the proverbial eel, and it usually took half the Washington team to bring him down.

Overall, the game was a success. It wasn't a 1902 blowout. Fans enjoyed the game. Tourists came to Pasa-dena. The Chamber of Commerce was happy. The Tour-nament of Roses Committee looked forward to another game, this time in the new Rose Bowl stadium under con-struction. The Rose Bowl parade had been a hit and the Elks could now rest, as could all the other participants.

THE ELKS MARCH 1916

The Brown players were gracious in defeat. They praised Washington as a tough team. Both teams attended a post-game party and then headed home. For the Cougars that meant a few more days of Hollywood shooting before heading back to Pullman where they had a victor's welcoming.

THE VICTORS

The boys from Providence headed home via San Francisco where they had a short stay. Then it was on two trains to the East Coast. There was one interesting change on this trek home. The two five-gallon glass containers that contained good old Rhode Island water were now filled with Napa Valley wine. Sadly, the players also received a crate of bad oranges that gave the players diarrhea. This, of course, proves that you can't have everything. Concerning another issue...The players had complained about the food on the way to Pasadena. To head off more complaints each player was given $21 for a food allowance. Each player would now purchase his own food. The players soon learned that there was always a saloon near a train depot. They would enter one and indulge at the free lunch counter. Many of the players arrived in Rhode Island with money still in their pockets. All and all things worked out.

ARRIVING IN SAN FRANCISCO

There was one unfortunate moment in the City by the Bay. Fritz Pollard was not given a room in the hotel where the team was staying. His teammates escorted him to a Black section of the city where he managed to get a room. He later said he was shaken by this experience. He also mentioned the two knife fights he witnessed. That night he placed a bureau against the door for security. `

Years later the Brown Bears would have a reunion.

THE 1916 BROWN UNIVERSITY TEAM REUNION

THE 1916 BROWN UNIVERSITY TEAM AS YOUNG MEN

As the train headed east Fritz Pollard could not have anticipated his enduring, long struggle to integrate professional football and to end the odious ban on Black players. All that was ahead of him. His life to this point was shaping him for that fight, as were the years ahead.

CHAPTER 14 – THE MEETING

February 25, 1933...Pittsburgh, Pennsylvania...The Fort Pitt Hotel... Eight men, all owners of professional football teams...An understanding arrived at...A dark period in NFL history inaugurated...

The Fort Pitt Hotel was located on the eastern edge of Pittsburgh Golden Triangle at Park Avenue and Tenth Street. Many considered the eight-story structure one the city's most elegant hotels. The hotel catered to the rich and famous, including William Jennings Bryan, Jack Benny, and Eleanor Roosevelt. The hotel was razed in 1967 to make way for the Penn Park development, but not the bitter memories of what took place there three decades earlier.

FORT PITT HOTEL

Four prominent NFL owners in particular attended the 1933 meeting: George Preston Marshall, George "Papa" Halas, Art Rooney, and Tim Mara. Art Rooney, the author of the Rooney Rule? No. That was the endeavor of his son. The meeting was to discuss league business. Careful notes were taken as their conversations focused on how to sustain professional football in the midst of the Great Depression. With millions out of work and money hard to come by game revenues were at risk. Eventually the discussions turned to another topic and the note taking stopped as an understanding was reached as to the future of the game. Two owners in particular convinced others to accept a fateful decision to ban Black players from the NFL.

MARSHALL   HALAS

ROONEY   MARA

For clarification...There exists no known document to prohibit Blacks from playing in the NFL. There are no known records of any direct conversations involving the owners and the ban. All owners attending the meeting denied the existence of a ban that existed from 1934 to 1946. A so-called Gentlemen's Agreement had been reached. But three things could not be denied. In 1933 there were two Black players in the NFL, Joe Lillard of the Chicago Cardinals and Ray Kemp of the Pittsburg Pirates (later the Steelers). They were the last Black players for twelve seasons. Also, no Black player donned an NFL uniform until Kenny Washington did so in 1946. Finally, Fritz Pollard spent a good deal of his life attempting to end the non-existent official ban that carried the weight of high tensile steel.

The football career of Kenny Washington of UCLA mirrored the odious exclusionary policy of the NFL.

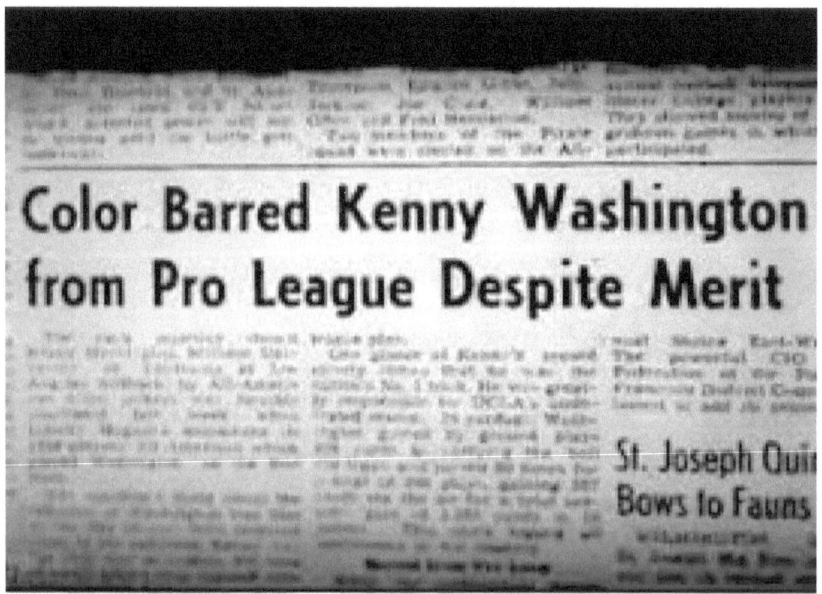

BANNED IN 1939

HIRED IN 1946 BY THE LOS ANGELES RAMS

George Preston Marshall is a curious figure in this saga. On the one hand he was an innovator who did much to improve the pro game. He realized that football was a form of entertainment and needed to emulate the college game with gala halftime shows and marching bands. As to the game itself he suggested a major change in the forward pass. Passes could be thrown from anywhere behind the line of scrimmage rather than at a minimum of five yards behind the line. He also called for the goal posts to be moved from the end line to the goal line to encourage field goals. That rule would be reversed in the 1970's to reduce the influence of the field goal. He pushed to standardize the game schedule so that each team played the same number of games. He encouraged splitting teams into divisions with the winners meeting in a championship. In some ways he was anticipating the future Super Bowl. He argued for gate receipts to be split between the home team and the visitors. He led the way with radio broadcasts of Sunday games to build interest in the sport and his team the Washington Redskins. The exploits of his team were broadcasted as far south as Florida. Since his team was the most southern team in the NFL this made commercial sense. To drum up business he scheduled preseason exhibition games in the South. Unfortunately, he chose a memorable fight song that epitomized his racial attitudes --- "Hail to the Redskins." It was, however, a song that appealed to white fans in the South.

> *Hail to the Redskins!*
> *Hail Victory!*
> *Brave on the Warpath!*
> *Fight for old D.C.!*
> *Run or pass and score --- we want a lot more!*
> *Beat 'em, Swamp 'em,*
> *Touchdown! --- Let the points soar!*
> *Fight on, fight on 'Til you have won*
> *Sons of Wash-ing-ton. Rah! Rah! Rah!*

The original first four lines were rather different before they were altered.

> *Hail to the Redskins!*
> *Hail Victory!*
> *Brave on the Warpath!*
> *Fight for old Dixie!*

The team's nickname was an insult to Native-Americans as were the lyrics to the fight song. The reference to Dixie suggests an admiration for the "Lost Cause" and the effort to perpetuate slavery in the Confederacy. The name would remain until more recent times. The word Dixie, however, was removed from the lyrics. Imbedded in the lyrics was a racial attitude toward Blacks that colored Marshall's life, but also reflected parts of the country, and to some extent Washington D.C. The capital was a segregated city in the 1930's with discriminatory policies in government and the private sector. Jim Crow reigned in the South and de facto discrimination was all too prevalent in the North, and a toxic mixture existed in D.C.

Marshall was born in Grafton, West Virginia in 1890. His family moved to Washington D.C. in 1910 where his father had a successful laundry business. Inheriting the business Preston Marshall became one of the wealthiest persons in the city. In time he bought a partial interest in the Boston Indians football team in 1925. After taking full control of ownership he moved the team to Washington and renamed it the Redskins. At the time he said the name was to honor his new football coach, William "Lone Star" Dietz, the former coach of the Washington State Cougars in the 1916 Rose Bowl, who claimed he was of Indian heritage.

WILLIAM "LONE STAR" DIETZ

Marshall was quoted as saying he would never hire a Black player. Amending that view slightly, he said he would sign a Black player "when the Harlem Globetrotters signed a white basketball player."

HARLEM GLOBETROTTERS   WASHINGTON GENERALS

The Globetrotters were first formed in 1926 on the South Side of Chicago where all the original players lived. They were originally called the Savoy Big Five. Since 1926 they have played in more than 26,000 exhibition games in 124 countries against a handpicked, less skilled team, the Washington Generals who acted as their foil. The Globetrotters combine theater, comedy, and athleticism to the joy of their fans. But make no mistake about it. The team could play ball. They won the World Professional Basketball Tournament in 1940. In 1948 they played a game that made the headlines. Up against the Minnesota Lakers, the best all-white team in professional basketball (NBA), they proved victorious. Indirectly their success spurred the recruitment of Black players in 1950. In that year the Boston Celtics drafted Chuck Cooper, a Globetrotter. He was the first Black player drafted by the NBA. Nat "Sweetwater" Clifton became the first Black player to sign an NBA contract after the New York Knicks purchased his contract from the Globetrotters.

The team's signature song was *Sweet Georgia Brown*. Freeman Davis first sang the lyrics. The Globetrotters adopted the music in 1952. Their theme song was played before every game. The lyrics were quite different than *Hail to the Redskins*.

> *Well let me tell you well no chick made*
> *Could be the same*
> *As sweet Georgia Brown*
> *Crazy feet that dance so neat*
> *Has sweet Georgia Brown*
> *Fella's sigh, and even cry*
> *For sweet Georgia Brown*
> *I tell you just why*
> *You know I don't lie*
> *It's been said*
> *She knocks them dead*
> *In any old town*
> *Since she came right*
> *It's a shame*
> *How she brings them down.*

Marshall's satirical comment played well with those opposed to integration. But, of course, he missed the larger picture. The Globetrotters proved that integrated basketball was possible and profitable, all that Fritz Pollard had been saying for years. If it was possible to do this on the basketball court than why not on the football field?

On another occasion Marshall said, "I am surprised that the world is on the brink of another war and they (critics) are worried about whether or not a Negro is going to play for the Redskins?" Again, he missed the mark. The looming war with

Nazi Germany and Imperial Japan would demand conscription of healthy young men for the armed forces. The draft did not discriminate. Blacks and whites would again be inducted into the services. Black inductees would be asked to fight for their country, even at a time when the racist policies of the Deep South confined them to second-class citizenship. In this Jim Crow laws mirrored to a degree Berlin's policies toward Jews. A Black playing for the Redskins was a sign of progress and paralleled the hope of Black soldiers that a post-war America would reward service with greater social justice and economic opportunity.

Marshall was also remarked that he "doubted the government had the right to tell the showman how to cast the play." In other words, he was in charge of his roster, not bureaucrats. In short, he was saying, "if I pay the salaries I can hire who I chose." Once more he missed the point. The private sector is not immune from public scrutiny and government oversight. That notion was proven during the Kennedy Administration. Marshall desperately needed to play in a new stadium that was in the works. He wanted a 30-year lease to play in Washington's new stadium. However, the new venue would be built on federally owned property. Marshall would get his lease if he integrated the team. In 1962 he bent. He reluctantly drafted Ernie Davis, the great Syracuse University runner. He was the top choice in the annual NFL draft. Davis balked. He wouldn't play for Marshall. Another deal was cut. Davis was traded to the Cleveland Browns for an all-pro, Bobby Mitchell. With that every NFL team now had at least one Black player.

THE END OF THE BAN – DAVIS AND MITCHELL

Marshall's bigotry extended even to his will and how his estate would disperse funds through the George Marshall Foundation, which had been set up to serve the interests of children in the Washington metropolitan area, but with one caveat. No money would go toward any purpose that supported the principal of racial integration in any form. After a protracted legal battle that demand was thrown out by the courts. Today the Foundation serves all children.

Whatever Marshall's involvement with the ban the role of other owners must be considered. They went along with the policy. They were complicit in the inclusionary but informal agreement. In 1963 the Pro Football Hall of Fame opened. Three former football owners were induct-ed in the inaugural class: George Halas, Tim Mara, and George Preston Marshall. All were present years earlier at the Fort Pitt Hotel on February 25, 1933 when the Gentle-men's Agreement was reached. It does not go unnoticed that the address of the Pro Football Hall of Fame is on George Halas Drive in Canton, Ohio. Jim Thorpe was also included in the inaugural class inducted in 1963. However, Fritz Pollard was not inducted that year. He would be in 2005, over 42-years later.

PRO FOOTBALL HALL OF FAME, CANTON, OHIO

Some years are more important than others. That was certainly true for Dan Reeves and the Cleveland Rams in 1945. He was the owner of the football team, which had just won the NFL championship game, 15 – 14 over the Washington Redskins. The coach of the Rams was Adam Walsh and he had been selected coach of the year by his peers. The Ram starting quarterback was a rookie from UCLA. His name was Bob Waterfield. He was the league's MVP. It appeared the Rams were a dynasty in the making.

DAN REEVES   BOB WATERFIELD   NFL CHAMPS

1945 CHAMPION CLEVELAND RAMS

Reeves, however, had three big problems. In dealing with them the Rams would usher in the integration of professional football. First, fan support for the championship team was tepid. Only 32,178 supported the championship game. Thousands of tickets went unsold. That had been all too true during the winning season. The Rams weren't drawing fans. They were playing their games in old League Stadium. The Cleveland Indians baseball team of the American League owned the venue. The Rams were renters. Some might call them orphans. The team wasn't making a profit. That was the real problem. Reeves felt the Rams didn't have a future in Cleveland. Reeves looked westward and to the untapped financial possibilities in California. Moving west was a radical notion. No team had ever won a championship in one city and then moved to another in the next year. In 1946 there was no professional baseball or football team west of the Mississippi River. Reeves and the Rams were moving into unknown territory.

Second, there was an upstart football conference, now competing with the NFL. This was the All-American Football Conference (AAFC). The new league played entertaining football, 1946-1949. The new Cleveland Browns were a charter member of the AAFC. Their coach was the legendary Paul Brown. In the first four seasons of the new league the Cleveland Browns compiled an enviable record, 47-4-3. The team won the AAFC championship each year. When the league folded in 1949 the Browns joined the NFL, along with the San Francisco 49ers and the original Baltimore Colts. The Browns won the NFL championship in their first year. They repeated in 1954, 1955, and 1964. Between 1965 and 1995 the Browns played in the NFL playoffs 14 times.

PAUL BROWN

MARION MOTLEY

Under Coach Brown the team competed with the Rams on another basis. In 1946 the Browns invited an unknown giant of a man who had played football at the University of Nevada and was on a service team during WWII. The coach of the service team was Paul Brown. Marion Motley tried out for the team and made it. In doing so he broke the color barrier and the NFL exclusionary policy. Motley played for seven seasons and set a record that still stands. He averaged 5.7 yards per carry. The great running back was the bruising heart of the Cleveland Browns. Though he was taunted with racial slurs and grudging hits on the field he gained 3,024 yards in his career. He once remarked: "They found out that while they were calling us n'ggers and alligator bait, I was running for touchdowns." That was Marion Motley and in the shadows, Fritz Pollard.

Whether it was his football intuition or a careful analysis of the AAFC Reeves knew it was time to depart Cleveland. The city couldn't support the Rams and the explosive Browns.

Assuming that the Rams would move to Los Angeles, Reeves faced another problem. Where would the Rams play? The Los Angeles Memorial Coliseum was the logical choice. To play in this famous venue a lease would need to be signed with the Coliseum Commission. In doing so Reeves, whether reluctantly or not, would undo the Gentlemen's Agreement still clinging to the NFL.

LOS ANGELES MEMORIAL COLISEUM

Dan Reeves expected little opposition in attaining a lease to the Los Angeles Memorial Coliseum. But that was before he ran into William Clair "Halley" Harding, a reporter for the *LA Tribune*, a respected Black owned newspaper. Harding was the sports editor of the paper. In his weekly columns he promoted the interests of Black athletes. He did so with unrelenting vigor and passion. He was following in the path of another newspaper sports writer, Fritz Pollard. As to Harding's background...He had played quarterback at Wilberforce University in Ohio. After graduation he briefly played basketball for the Harlem Rens (short for Renaissance). This basketball team was the predecessor of the Harlem Globetrotters. Harding also played baseball for the Kansas City Monarchs in the Negro league. One of his teammates was Satchel Paige.

During the Second World War his determination to seek social justice was eloquently stated in one of his columns. Conscripting Blacks and then denying them opportunities in the services and at home in peacetime pursuits was unacceptable to Harding.

I wonder if the powers that be in baseball know that a speeding bullet does NOT veer when it gets to a colored person; nor does a bomb from a plane fail to explode simply because the target turns out to be colored soldiers. It is high time that the same people who unhesitatingly ask them to sacrifice their lives in times of war fix it so that in times of peace, this liberty they are supposed to have bled and died for becomes reality.

On January 14, 1946 Ram executives went before the Coliseum Commission to seek a long-term lease. It was a forgone conclusion that the Commission would grant the lease. After all, Los Angeles would be gaining an excellent professional football team and the Coliseum would have a profitable client. Again, the expectation was that the Commission would rubber stamp the deal. Of course that was before Harding weighed in with a counter argument. Basically, he argued that the Coliseum was publically owned property supported by the taxpayers, both Black and white. That being the situation the Commission should not grant a lease unless and until the Ram executives promised to integrate the team. He argued:

We all know that baseball is a national sport and that football is its neglected stepchild everywhere except here in Los Angeles. We have two fine semipro football teams here, the Hollywood Bears and the Los Angeles Bulldogs. We have players of all races and creeds on those teams. It is our way here in the west to give every person a chance to succeed and excel.

All those in attendance gave their full attention as Harding continued.

You can do this at the college level. Three quarters of UCLA's 1939 backfield were Negroes. We have always had integrated teams out here in the west. But unfortunately this is not the case everywhere in our great nation. Today, you will not see a Negro on any NFL football field.

Harding was referencing the UCLA trio of Woody Strode, Jackie Robinson and Kenny Washington.

STRODE, ROBINSON, WASHINGTON IN 1939.

Harding added in caustic terms that the only Negroes in the NFL were the janitors and water boys. That said, he moved on to the salient issue for the Commission.

The NFL is segregated and has barred Negro players since 1933. It wasn't always that way. We had many, many Negro ballplayers before that fateful year. Charles Follis...Rube Marshall...Fritz Pollard...and Ray Kemp, who was the last Negro player in the NFL before the door was closed. There hasn't been another now for thirteen years.

RAY KEMP

Without saying it directly Harding was putting a difficult question before the Commission. Did the City of Los Angeles want to continue the exclusionary policy? If so, was the Commission complicit in maintaining a racist, discriminatory policy? The unstated questions lingered in the air. Harding next gave those in attendance a history lesson.

It's a shame. America fought Adolf Hitler because he was a racial supremacist, yet our Army is still segregated. We fought the Civil War against those who believed that Negroes should be enslaved and excluded from society, yet exclusion still exists. Even our Declaration of Independence tells us that all men are created equal, yet opportunity is still not equal.

Then Harding said quietly but in thundering words:

We cannot allow a segregated NFL team to use a stadium paid for by our taxes. We cannot play segregated football here in Los Angeles. It's just not our way. I oppose any team that will not give our citizens an opportunity to try out, an opportunity to be included, and an opportunity to play.

Harding's words had the desired affect. The Commission hesitated. The expected smooth sailing the Rams had expected was called into question. The Rams' general manager was stunned by the turn of events. Chile Walsh was in a vice. The Rams needed to extricate themselves from Cleveland. The Coliseum was a prerequisite to such a move. The proverbial ball was in the Rams' hands. What would Reeves' team do? Reluctantly, the Rams caved. Walsh said, "Any qualified Negro football player is invited by me at this moment to try out for the Los Angeles Rams." Harding heard the words and then pushed an additional demand that went beyond a verbal commitment. He demanded that the Rams' commitment to integrating the team be a part of any lease agreement. That demand was taken under consideration by the Commission. The Rams were coming to LA.

The onerous ban was gone. The NFL had turned a corner. The dreams of Fritz Pollard were about to be realized. The Cleveland Browns were coming to Los Angeles. The team would be integrated.

A short time later the Rams made history. On March 21, 1946, only three months after Harding's impassioned speech, Kenny Washington signed a contract with the Rams. It included a "no cut clause" to make sure the Rams wouldn't use the signing as a publicity stunt. Soon afterwards Woody Strode, Washington's teammate at UCLA, was offered a contract. The team would be integrated. The NFL racist policy was no more. Fritz Pollard's hopes had finally been realized.

Tim Mara was the owner of the New York Giants. Though originally reluctant to see the Rams go to Los Angeles and to offer contracts to Washington and Strode, he now openly praised the deal, saying:

We can't lose on that move. Both are good football players and both will be real attractions. I am sure we will get thousands of more Negro fans to attend the games at the Polo Grounds this year because they will have an added interest in the league.

Los Angeles played up the deal. The Rams, however, and the NFL said little in public beyond a curious disclaimer.

The National Football League has never had a rule against the use of Negro players and no precedent is being set in the signing of Washington and Strode.

An aside… The Rams were concerned that Washington would be the only Black on the team and in the entire NFL. To alleviate that concern they signed Woody Strode, Washington's teammate from UCLA. And then a problem arose. It turned out that Strode was married to a beautiful Hawaiian. Some Ram executives wanted to cut Strode because of this. Apparently Dan Reeves didn't approve of Strode's wife and Hawaiian life style. The wife was Luana and she was a descendent of Liliuokalani, the last Queen of the Kingdom of Hawaii. Strode met her in 1938 when he played in the Pineapple Bowl in Hawaii. Rather than living in a Black neighborhood in Los Angeles, Strode and his wife chose to live among a community of Pacific Islander entertainers in the Hollywood area. Seemingly Reeves felt awkward about this. He never explained why. When Washington heard that Strode would be cut because of Reeve's concerns, he said: "If I can't have Woody, you can't have me." The Rams deferred to Washington. Strode remained on the team. Reeves, it should be noted, never knew that Strode's background included a most interesting fact; he was part Indian, a member of the Blackfeet tribe.

As it turns out Woody Strode had two careers, one in football and the other in action movies.

THE PROFESSIONALS   THE MAN WHO SHOT LIBERTY VANCE

SERGEANT RUTLEDGE

The second shoe fell on April 10, 1947. Jackie Robinson signed a contract with the Brooklyn Dodgers. Another color barrier was broken. Some sport historians believe that Washington's signing with the Rams "tipped Branch Rickey to do what he did with Robinson." The signing of a Black football player took the pressure off the Brooklyn Dodgers. The country was moving on.

JACKIE ROBINSON AND BRANCH RICKEY

As to Halley Harding…He left the *Los Angeles Tribune* to work for the competition, the *Los Angeles Sentinel*. He later moved to Chicago where he wrote for several weeklies, including the *New Crusader*. Little is known about his personal life. He worked at that weekly for fifteen years before dying in 1967 from a stroke. One thing is known, however, about his days in Chicago. He continuously pushed the Chicago Cubs to sign their first Black baseball player. That player was Ernie Banks.

ERNIE BANKS

One of Harding's peers recounted how this crusader for social justice began each day. It appeared that he "got up each morning and proceeded to put on his boxing gloves as soon as he had shaved and showered, to get ready to battle them and their prejudices." In that, he was kin to Fritz Pollard.

HALLEY HARDING, THE CRUSADER

THE POST-GAME SHOW

I'm so glad I went, because I was the only repre-sentative there from our family. I got there and I'll never forget walking in that door and I saw the four pictures of the four inductees and my knees almost buckled.

Stephen Towns, grandson of Fritz Pollard, at the Pro Football Hall of Fame enshrinement, August 7, 2005, in Canton, Ohio

In his last days Fritz Pollard went to live with his son, Fritz Pollard, Jr. and his wife in Silver Springs, Maryland. He was approaching his ninety-second birthday and was in failing heath. He had contracted pneumonia and was admitted to the Silver Springs Hospital. On May 11, 1988 he died. At the time Fritz Pollard Jr. said this of his father's small size as a football player: "A guy that did ev-erything he did and did it in the way he did it, he couldn't be small. He was larger than life in a sense. He was that way until he died." Pollard was cremated at the Fort Lincoln Cemetery in Brentwood, Maryland. Three daughters survived him and one son, Fritz Jr.

Fritz was immensely proud of him, especially for winning a bronze medal in the 110-meter hurdles in the 1936 Olympics and for his military service during WWII.

FRITZ POLLARD, JR.

CHAPTER 16 – THE ROONEY RULE

The death of Fritz Pollard did not end his effort to in-tegrate professional football. In his name the Fritz Pollard Alliance Foundation was formed in 2003 as a non-prof-it with the expressed purpose to champion diversity and equality in the NFL. It was named after Pollard for his earlier efforts to achieve this goal. The Alliance pushes team owners to make sure that promotions and opportu-nities are offered to all competent applicants regardless of ethnicity or race. Job opportunities include assistant and head coaching positions and front office manage-ment. This advocacy leads to an uneasy relationship with the Commissioner's Office, as well as the owners. Each year the Alliance honors those individuals who exhibited strength, courage, and inclusiveness to achieve diversity and fairness, all traits of Fritz Pollard.

The awards for 2023 went to the following. The Salute to Excellence Award went to Leslie Frazier, the defensive coordinator of the Buffalo Bills. Sharing the award was Perry Fewell, the Senior Vice President of NFL Officiating. The award honored their exceptional performances to achieve diversity. The John B. Wooten Award went the San Francisco 49ers for taking extraordinary steps to hire candidates of color. The collegiate award went to Deslin Alexandra, a student-athlete whose performance on and off the field was in the spirit of Fritz Pollard. The most prestigious award went to Kevin Demoff, the Chief Operating Officer of the Los Angeles Rams for his dedication to improving the football workplace.

The Daniel M. Rooney Lifetime Achievement Award recognized his efforts.

KEVIN DEMOFF

Rod Graves was the Director of the Fritz Pollard Alliance. At the awards ceremony he clearly stated the continuing goal of the Alliance.

"Our mantra is to resist the status quo of diversity hiring practices in the NFL, as we build bridges and navigate barriers. Although the doors are open to ownership conversations in many cases, the results remain barren of inclusive successes. The Alliance continues to support a key factor in its efforts to achieve diversity, the Rooney Rule."

The Rooney Rule was set up in 2003. It was named after Dan Rooney, the late son of the original owner of the Pittsburgh Steelers, and who was also the former chairman of the NFL's diversity committee. The Rule was created in response to the 2002 firings of Tony Dungy of the Tampa Bay Buccaneers and Dennis Green of the Minnesota Vikings. They were fired even though they had winning records and had proved to be outstanding coaches. Many in the sporting world cried "foul."

DAN ROONEY

TONY DUNGY

DENNIS GREEN

One catalyst for the heated response was an academic study that pointed out that in the NFL:

. Blacks were less likely to be hired, but more likely to be fired, especially for head coaching positions.
. 60% of the players were men of color.
. only 9% of head coaches were Black.
. only 35% of assistance coaches were Black.
. of 32 offensive coordinators, 2 represented minorities

Why was this the situation? The answer was simple. The NFL ownership structure was at the root of the problem. Owners controlled all decisions made by management and coaches. Owners tended to be older white men. The average age in 2003 was 69 with 7 owners older than 75. As the argument went they came of age before the recent civil rights movement. They had positions of authority and great wealth. They also perpetuated systemic racism that suppressed mobility for the Black workforce in the NFL. This led to only one conclusion. The owners saw Black players as a means to an end. They produced a product for owners to sell. That being the case the owners were disingenuous in their professed efforts for diversity. The Rooney Rule attempted to remedy this situation by requiring at least one member of each offensive coaching staff be either an ethic minority or a woman. The same requirement applied to all coaching positions, including head coach. Essentially this was a mandate to ensure a minority individual would be considered for a position.

Has the Rooney Rule worked? Has the rule developed a deep and talented pool of prospective candidates for all NFL positions? Many would argue yes, but to only a limited degree. It should not be forgotten that even before the Rooney Rule there were two Black coaches in the NFL. The first was, of course, Fritz Pollard. The second was Art Shell of the Los Angeles Raiders (1989-1994). Shell was highly successful. He compiled a record of 54 wins and 38 losses. In 1990 he was the American Football Conference (AFC) Coach of the Year. With a 12-4 record the Raiders advanced to the AFC championship game. In doing this Shell became the first Black head coach to do so. As a player and coach he left his mark, as did Pollard with the Akron Pros years earlier.

ART SHELL

The record of Black NFL head football coaches in recent times is shown below. The list does not include interim coaches.

COACH	TEAM	RECORD
ART SHELL	LOS ANGELES RAIDERS	56-52
DENNIS GREEN	MINNESOTA VIKINGS	113-94
RAY RHODES	PHILADELPHIA EAGLES GREEN BAY PACKERS	37-42-1
TONY DUNGY	TAMPA BAY BUCCANEERS INDIANAPOLIS COLTS	148-79
HERMAN EDWARDS	NEW YORK JETS	56-78
MARVIN LEWIS	CINCINNATI BENGALS	131-129
LOVIE SMITH	CHICAGO BEARS	95-103

ROMEO CRENNEL	CLEVELAND BROWNS KANSAS CITY CHIEFS HOUSTON TEXANS	32-63
MIKE TOMLIN	PITTSBURGH STEELERS	163-93
MIKE SINGLETARY	SAN FRANCISCO 49ers	18-22
JIM CALDWELL	INDIANAPOLIS COLTS DETROIT LIONS	64-54
LESLIE FRAZIER	MINNESOTA VIKINGS	21-32-1

HERMAN EDWARDS

ROMEO CRENNEL

LOVIE SMITH

MARVIN LEWIS

JIM CALDWELL   MIKE SINGLETARY   LESLIE FRAZIER

The record of these coaches indicated four things. First, there were talented Black applicants for NFL head coaching positions. Second, once hired they could field winning teams. Third, the Rooney Rule was needed to provide Black assistant coaches an opportunity to become head coaches. Forth, the owners needed to make a good faith effort to hire competent people regardless of their ethnicity or race in supporting the Rooney Rule. In the meantime the NFL needed to deal with other related racial issues.

NFL: CALLING THE PLAYS HIRES BETWEEN 2012-2021	WHITE	PEOPLE OF COLOR
HEAD COACHES	51	11
GENERAL MANAGERS	31	6

DATA DOWNLOAD — 2021 NFL DIVERSITY AND INCLUSION REPORT

CHAPTER 17 – MEXICO CITY

Some years are more challenging than others. That was true in 1968 when the country was going through dramatic and turbulent events. There were the two assassinations. On April 4, 1968 Martin Luther King was killed. Violent riots erupted, especially in Washington D.C., Baltimore, and Chicago. Racial tensions increased as over 40 people were killed during a month of protests. In response the landmark Civil Rights Act of 1968 was passed with bipartisan Congressional support. In November Robert Kennedy was struck down in California. As in the case of King, the killer wanted to alter history. He did. Abroad the country was bogged down in Vietnam with over 500,000 troops involved in a war of choice. The Tet Offensive on January 30, 1968 brought things to a boiling point with anti-war demonstrations on college campuses and in the streets. In many ways it seemed like the country was a war with itself. In the fall the traumatic months came to a head in the most unlikely of places, Mexico City, where the 1968 Summer Olympics were held.

MARTIN LUTHER KING JR.   **ROBERT KENNEDY**

The date was October 16, 1968. The sprinters, youthful, muscular, and fast listened intently for the starter's gun, each man posed after years of training for the mad dash ahead of him. Then it came…A blast into the rarified air of Mexico City and the runners were off. Twenty seconds later the race was over. An American, Tommie Smith had set a world record time for the 200-meter event, 19.83 seconds. Another American John Carlos finished third in a time of 20.10 seconds. Sandwiched between them was an Australian. His name was Peter Newman. His time was 20.06 seconds.

TOMMIE SMITH WINS

After the race, with the Olympic crowd still awed by the record-breaking speed, the three men congratulated each other in the spirit of the ancient Greeks. Then it was time for the medal ceremony. The three men climbed onto the podiums. They were awarded their medals, gold for Smith, silver for Norman, and bronze for Carlos. They stood quietly and waited for the playing of the national anthem of the United States, patriotic music to celebrate the winner's country. The recorded music began and unexpectedly the two Black runners from America raised gloved-fists into the sky as the Star Spangled Banner was played. The moment has come to symbolize the most overtly political statement in the history of the modern Olympics and in doing so they set off a controversy that continues to this day.

DEMONSTRATING

The two American athletes received their medals shoeless. They wore only black socks. This was not by accident. The absence of shoes represented the impoverishment of Blacks citizens and the poverty that oppressed their lives. Around his neck Smith wore a black scarf to symbolized "Black Pride." Carlos' tracksuit top was unzipped to show Black solidarity with blue-collared workers in the U.S. Carlos also wore a necklace of beads, which, as he later said, was to remember those who were lynched or killed over the years. It was also for those thrown off the side of slave ships in the Middle Passage between Africa and the Western Hemisphere. All three of the runners wore the Olympic Project for Human Rights badges (OPHR). Why the Australian? Norman was a critic of Australia's White Australia

Policy and very sympathetic with the actions of Smith and Carolos.

Was the demonstration staged? Simply put, yes. By way of example… The Americans planned to bring black gloves to the event. Carlos, however, forgot his in the Olympic Village. Norman suggested that Carlos wear Smith's left-handed glove. Because of this Carlos raised his left hand as opposed to his right, thereby differing from the traditional Black Power salute.

As they left the Olympic podium the two Americans were booed. Much later Smith said of the moment, "If I win, I am an American, not a Black American. But if I did something bad then they would say 'a Negro.' We are Black and we are proud of being Black. Black America will understand." He also pointed out that he was concerned about the lack of Black assistant coaches in professional football and how Muhammad Ali was stripped of his title. He mentioned the lack of decent housing for Blacks and the fact that Black kids were not able to attend top colleges and universities. The immediate response to the 'raised fist" was sharp and unrelenting. *Time Magazine* stated on October 25, 1968: "Faster, Higher, Stronger is the motto of the Olympics. Angrier, nastier, uglier better describes the scene in Mexico City last week." Others described Smith and Carlos as a "couple of black-skinned storm troopers, who were ignoble, juvenile and unimaginative."

Both Smith and Carlos had to endure abuse and they and their families received death threats, but the worst criticism came from an American within the Olympic family. That was Avery Brundage, who was the President of the International Olympic Committee (IOC). He described the actions of Smith and Carlos as "a deliberate and violent breach of the fundamental principles of the Olympic spirit." He deemed their actions "as a domestic political statement unfit for the apolitical international forum the Olympic games were intended to be." In addition, he described the Smith-Carlos incident as "Warped mentalities and cracked personalities that seem to be everywhere and impossible to eliminate." He maintained that the incident was the "nasty demonstration against the American flag by negroes." He ordered Smith and Carlos suspended from the US team and banned from the Olympic Village. The US Olympic Committee refused to do so. Brundage then threatened to ban the entire US team. Under this pressure the two athletes were expelled from the Games. The IOC did not force Smith and Carlos to return their medals. It should be noted that in 1936 Brundage did not object to Nazi salutes during the Berlin Games. He made the curious argument in 1968 that the Nazi salute was a national salute representing the German nation and was acceptable. The salute of Smith and Carolos was not that of a nation and was therefore unacceptable. Brundage made a convenient, if not bigoted distinction.

AVERY BRUNDAGE

Sometimes forgotten in the drama of the time was that three other Black athletes demonstrated: Lee Evans, Larry James and Ron Freeman. Apparently Evans, along with Tommie Smith, was the force behind the protests. Evans (gold), James (silver) and Freeman (bronze) took the top three medals in the 400 meter finals. They all wore black berets on the podium in imitation of the Black Panther Party.

The three men, along with Vince Matthews, also won the 4 X 400 meter relay in the time of 2:56.16, a world record that lasted 24-years.

THE VICTORS

Overlooked in this whole business was Peter Newman. He was severely reprimanded by the Australian Olympic Committee and criticized in his country's conservative newspapers. He was not sent to the 1972 Olympic games even though he had better qualifying times than many others. During the 1972 Olympics in Sydney he was not invited to take part in the celebration. All this, it appears, because he was sympathetic to his competitor's protests. When he died in 2006 two of his pallbearers were Tommie Smith and John Carlos.

THE PROTESTERS

What took place in Mexico was long ago, and is still relevant in more recent times when two football players decided to protest racism in the country.

CHAPTER 18 – PROTEST

It was just another pre-season game in the NFL pitting the San Francisco 49ers against the Green Bay Packers in Levi Stadium. It was just another pre-season game to give the coaches another chance to check up on the vets and to give a closer look at the rookies. It was just another pre-season game for Packer and 49er faithful, a moment to cheer for their guys. Just another game only it wasn't and because it wasn't history was altered ever so slightly. Just prior to the kickoff an ancient ritual dating back to the Romans was once again repeated. On the fifty yard line the American flag was present and soon the Star Spangle Banner's patriotic words took to the heavens. Thousands of fans stood and even a few sang the national anthem. Many men took off their hats and held them over their hearts out of a deep respect for those who had made the ultimate sacrifice to preserve out liberties. A few wearing military uniforms snapped to attention and saluted the flag they had sworn to protect. Players, coaches, and other personnel also stood quietly. That is, all but two players. The media spotted two red-clad 49ers sitting quietly during the pre-game ritual and then kneeling. Their names are now part of NFL history and much more: Colin Kaepernick and Eric Reid.

REID AND KAEPERNICK

When asked why he didn't stand Kaepernick said he was responding to the deaths of Alton Sterling in Louisiana and Philando Castile in Minnesota, both at the hands of police officers. He believed, as he pointed out, that the police should be held accountable for killing citizens. He felt he needed to urge white Americans to "look at themselves in the mirror after centuries of being able ignore the plight of Black Americans." He further stated the police were supposed to protect us, not murder us, and that's what the issue really is and we need to change that."

ALTON STERLING   PHILANDO CASTILE

He further stated the police "shouldn't be able to kill unarmed Black people without consequence." He also pointed out:

... that what was done was controversial but only for those who see controversy in asking for basic human rights for Blacks that allegedly were afforded to them under the 14th Amendment nearly two centuries ago.

Continuing to respond to the media he said. "I'm not going to stand up to show pride in a flag for a country that oppressed Black people and people of color." He also drew a line between his professional football career and what was really at stake.

To me this is bigger than football and it would be selfish on my part to look the other way. There are bodies in the street and people getting paid leave and getting away with murder.

PROTESTS IN THE STREETS

———————

What happened to Alton Sterling? He was a 37-year old Black man who was shot and killed by two Baton Rouge police officers in Louisiana. The date was July 5, 2016. The officers stated they were trying to control the man's arms outside of a convenience store where he had used a gun to threaten a man. According to the police Sterling was reaching for a loaded handgun in his pocket as they attempted to subdue him. The U.S. Department of Justice investigated the death and decided that no charges would be filed against the officers involved. The same conclusion was reached by the Attorney General's office in Louisiana. The officers had "acted in a reasonable and justifiable manner." Five years after the shooting the family of Alton Sterling settled a wrongful death suit. The family was awarded $4.5 million settlement. This closed the case but not the anger many felt.

———————

Again, what happened to Philando Castile? On July 6, 2016 he was fatally shot by an officer of the St. Anthony Police Department. He had been pulled over around 9:00 p.m. in Falcon Heights, a suburb of Saint Paul, Minnesota. At the time he was traveling with his girlfriend and her four-year old daughter. After showing his license and registration things got out of control concerning a firearm he was licensed to carry. An officer fired seven close range shots. Castile died about an hour later from his wounds at Hennepin County Medical Center. The officer was later charged with second-degree manslaughter and two counts of dangerous discharge of a weapon. Eventually a jury acquitted him of all charges. Following that the officer was immediately fired by the City of Saint Anthony. After bringing a wrongful death lawsuit against the City the family settled for $3.8 million. To a degree all of this was played out in street protests.

Apparently the two shootings played on Eric Reid. After the kneeling episode he put into words the "why" of the protest. It was about injustice, racial profiling, police brutality, and a broken criminal justice system. It was never about the flag or the military as many critics claimed. Reid agreed with his teammate when he said:

The media painted this as I'm anti-American, anti-men and women of the military, and that's not the case at all. I realize that men and women of the military go out and sacrifice their selves in harm's way for my freedoms of speech and my freedoms in this country, and my freedom to take a seat or take a knee, so I have the utmost respect for them and I think what I did was taken out of context and spun a different way.

He added:

In respecting such principles as freedom of religion and freedom of expression, we recognize the right of an individual to choose to participate or not in our celebration of the national anthem.

It is teasing to consider what Fritz Pollard would have thought about this protest. Certainly, he would have been sympathetic. Decades earlier he had fought against the same race-based attitudes and policies that demeaned Blacks, whether on the athletic field or on city streets. At the same time he tended to be conservative in his politics and a staunch supporter of the military. Taking all this into account he might have sought a middle ground, as he always did, in order to survive in a white society. He would have desired the same goals but in a protest less overtly objectionable to many.

The general response to the "kneeing" was immediate and disheartening. Both men received death threats. Many referred to them as traitors. Some took umbrage at the accusations of racism. Others simply didn't want a political statement at the game. They just wanted a day off from our divisive politics. Kaepernick in particular quickly became persona nongrata just three years after leading the 49ers to a Super Bowl.

The response of the NFL was equivocal and prudent. Some sort of compromise or middle ground was needed. The league was in a tough spot. On the one hand it didn't want to antagonize its fan base. On the other hand, 70% or more of the players were Black. Though sympathetic to the aims of the protest, the NFL would encourage but not require players to stand during the playing of the national anthem. If that was not acceptable players could remain off the field until the ceremony concluded. So to speak, out of sight, out of mind. Polls taken at the time suggested the obvious. Americans were divided by age and political party affiliation on the question of kneeling as a form of protest. Overall there was considerable support for the protest that increased as additional police shootings occurred.

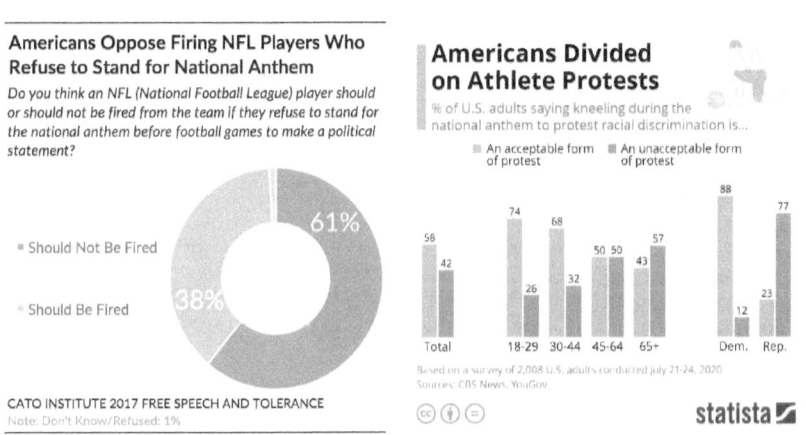

Americans Oppose Firing NFL Players Who Refuse to Stand for National Anthem

Do you think an NFL (National Football League) player should or should not be fired from the team if they refuse to stand for the national anthem before football games to make a political statement?

- Should Not Be Fired **61%**
- Should Be Fired **38%**

CATO INSTITUTE 2017 FREE SPEECH AND TOLERANCE
Note: Don't Know/Refused: 1%

Americans Divided on Athlete Protests

% of U.S. adults saying kneeling during the national anthem to protest racial discrimination is...

- An acceptable form of protest
- An unacceptable form of protest

	Total	18-29	30-44	45-64	65+	Dem.	Rep.
Acceptable	58	74	68	50	57	88	23
Unacceptable	42	26	32	50 43	43	12	77

Based on a survey of 2,008 U.S. adults conducted July 21-24, 2020
Sources: CBS News, YouGov

statista

Unfortunately President Trump got involved in the national discussion, if not debate. Before his base supporters in Alabama he challenged the league's owners "to release anyone who engages in the movement started by former San Francisco 49er quarterback Colin Kaepernick." He added: "Wouldn't you love to see one of the NFL owners, when somebody disrespects our flag, to say, 'Get that soon of a bitch off the field right now. Out! He's fired. He's fired!'"

The nation's leader went on to say:

If a player wants the privilege of making millions of dollars in the NFL or other leagues, he or she should not be allowed to disrespect our Great American Flag and should stand for the National Anthem. If not, YOU'RE FIRED. Find something else to do.

The NFL Commissioner, Roger Goodell, pushed back against the President, stating:

The NFL and our players are at our best when we help create a sense of unity in our country and our culture. Divisive comments like these demonstrate an unfortunate lack of respect for the NFL, our great game, and all our players, and a failure to understand the overwhelming force for good our clubs and players represent in our communities.

The Executive Director of the NFL Players Association also joined in the fray, stating, "the union will never back down when it comes to protecting the constitutional rights of our players as citizens as well as their safety as men who compete in a game that exposes them to great risks."

To some extent the debate continues to this day.

The debate took an unfortunate turn. Kaepernick was a free agent the next year and was not rehired by the 49ers or any other team, even though he was a quality QB who would help any team. This led to a legal suit against the NFL and a potential court trial. The charge was straightforward. The owners were blackballing the protester because of his actions. A gentlemen's agreement had been reached to exclude him from playing in the NFL. Again, nothing was in writing. No conversations had been taped. It was once more the stuff Fritz Pollard had fought against but was unable to document with written records.

The NFL fought back. The last thing the league wanted was a public trial. Such a public hearing might prove embarrassing, especially if a full investigation proved Kaepernick was right. A jury might find for the plaintiff resulting in a huge financial award. The NFL wanted to avoid this. The owners wanted the case settled through arbitration, a process that worked to their advantage. The union contract stipulated that a player had to prove the owners conspired against him, always a difficult thing to do in the absence of written records or some sort of conclusive evidence of collusion.

A surprised secret agreement was reached that ended the suit. All pending grievances were resolved. The confidentiality agreement reached meant that all discussion and debate ceased. There would be no trial. There would be no future arbitration. Speculation was rife as to the details of the agreement. Was there a large payout of Kaepernick's contract? Would other players maintain their professional careers if they had joined in the protests? In the end the agreement went along with the latest NFL policy incarnation. Players must stay in the locker room during the playing of the national anthem if they were not going to stand as Old Glory was celebrated. The player's union supported the agreement, stating:

We are not privy to the details of the settlement, but support the decision by the players and their counsel. We conscientiously supported Colin and Eric from the start of their protests, participated with their lawyers throughout their legal proceedings and were prepared to participate in the upcoming trial in pursuit of both truth and justice for what we believe the NFL and its clubs did to them. We are glad that Eric has earned a job and a new contract with the Carolina Panthers and we continue to hope that Colin gets his opportunity as well.

Seen in a larger framework Kaepernick's protest symbolized his right under the Constitution to speak his mind. In 1943 Justice Robert Jackson explained this right to dissent in West Virginia State Board of Education v. Barnette. In his majority opinion he wrote:

If there is any fixed star in our constitutional constellation, it is that no official, high or petty, can prescribe what shall be orthodox in politics, nationalism, religion, or other matters of opinion or force citizens to confess by word or act their faith within.

He added as a society we should not coerce uniformity of sentiment in support of some end thought essential at the time. We must be careful to avoid eliminating dissent because, as often happens, we soon are eliminating the dissenters. The First Amendment was designed to avoid this. Our public officials must trust the citizens to make their own choices about whom and what to believe. Justice Jackson spoke to these points in the midst of a war against totalitarian Nazi Germany, where dissent was not permitted, even punishable by death. At the conclusion of the war he was appointed the Chief Justice at the Nuremberg Trials, where Nazi leaders were put on trial for their crimes against humanity.

JUSTICE JACKSON AND PROTESTS

In short, Colin Kaepernick and Eric Reid had a right to protest racial injustice. In doing so they also had to deal with sharp criticism, whether deserved or not. The media saw to that.

CHAPTER 19 – ALLEGATIONS

One could say the whole business began with a text message from one football guy to another. But it hap-pened on January 27, 2022.

Belichick: Sounds like you have landed --- congrats!

Flores: Did you hear something I didn't?

Belichick: Giants???

Flores: I interviewed on Thursday. I think I have a shot at it.

Belichick: Got it --- I hear from Buffalo and NYG that you are their guy. Hope it works out for you.

Flores: That's definitely what I want! I hope you're right coach. Thank you. Coach, are you talking to Brian Flores or Brian Daboll? Just making sure.

Belichick: Sorry --- I fucked this up. I double-checked and misread the text. I think they are naming Daboll. Sorry about that. BB

Flores: Thanks Bill.

BRIAN FLORES

BILL BELICHICK

BRIAN DABOLL

Just a few words between buddies... Just a few words to inflame the NFL with still another lawsuit...Just a few words to call into question whether the NFL was truly committed to diversity for head coaches and those in management. Belichick's honest mistake was like a shot fired in the night. The issue here was that the New York Giants had already decided on their next coach days before Brian Flores had an opportunity for an interview. The Giant's management hadn't given Flores a real chance. The interview process was a sham. This occurred despite the NFL's Rooney Rule meant to curb this sort of thing. For Flores it was incredibly frustrating, if not insulting and raised again the question of whether systemic racism still haunted the league.

Brian Flores decided to fight back. He would take on the NFL and its hiring practices, especially where people of color were involved. As had Fritz Pollard and Colin Kaepernick, Flores was determined to vanquish the status quo that maintained discriminatory hiring practices, even at the expense of his own coaching career.

Flores sued three teams, including the Miami Dolphins, the Denver Broncos, and the New York Giants on February 1, 2022. He alleged discrimination regarding his interviews with Denver and the Giants in addition to being fired by Miami. The 58-page lawsuit was filed in a Manhattan federal court. The suit seeks class-action status. The heart of the suit rests on the e-mail between Flores and Belichick. According to Flores he received numerous text messages from the New England coach with whom he had worked for ten years as a Patriot assistant coach. Flores asserted that Belichick had heard from "Buffalo and NYG that you are their guy." As already noted Flores asked for clarification. Which Brian was Belichick talking about, Brian

Flores or Brian Daboll, who was also in the running for the New York Giant job? In response Belichick acknowledged his mistake and informed Flores that Daboll was getting the job. That being the case Flores argued that his in-person with the Giants, while it fulfilled the Rooney Rule, was nevertheless a farce since the club had already decided on Daboll. In sum Flores contended that the Giants only interviewed him in order to show that management was in compliance with the Rooney Rule requiring at least one minority candidate being interviewed in person. For the NFL it was another Kaepernick challenge.

Concerning the Miami Dolphins… Flores alleged in his suit that he was "incentivized" by management to "tank" or to purposely lose games, shortly after he was hired in 2019. The pressure came from Stephen Ross, the owner of the team. Flores alleges he was offered $100,000 for each game the team lost. Why the bonus? The owner didn't want to compromise Miami's chance for a high draft choice. Flores stated that his team never lost a game on purpose. Because of that Flores contended he was seen as "noncompliant and difficult to work with." He was also treated with distain. The Dolphins vehemently denied the allegations against them. They noted they were "proud of the diversity and inclusion throughout their organization."

The team said, "The implication that we acted in a manner inconsistent with the integrity of the game is incorrect."

Concerning the New York Giants... The team pushed back against Flores' charges, stating the team was "pleased and confident" with their hiring practices." Moreover management said:

We interviewed an impressive and diverse group of candidates. The fact of the matter is, Brian Flores was in the conversation to be our head coach until the eleventh hour. Ultimately, we hired the individual we felt was most qualified for the job.

Concerning the Denver Broncos...Again management stated it had given Flores a fair and impartial hearing. According to the team Flores had a 3 1/2-hour interview with five Bronco executives on January 5, 1919 in Providence, Rhode Island. They contended that:

Pages of detailed notes, analysis and evaluations from our interview demonstrate the depth of our conversation and sincere interest in Mr. Flores as a head coach candidate. Our process was thorough and fair to determine the most qualified candidate for our head coaching position. The Broncos will vigorously defend the integrity and values of our organization --- and its employees --- from such baseless and disparaging claims.

In response, Wigdor Law L.I.P., the legal firm representing Flores, said the coach hopes to "shine a light on the racial injustices that take place inside the NFL." Implied by the suit was that Black coaches are paid less and fired more quickly than white coaches even when their job performance was better. Hovering in the background was the shadow of institutional racism and the role of owners in the hiring process. For example:

Do owners have less patience with nonwhite NFL coaches?

Do owners feel more comfortable with white coaches?

Do owners have higher, if not almost impossible expectations for non-white coaches?

The questions posed are difficult to answer. This is partially true because the NFL is a unique enterprise. A small monopoly of owners can essentially agree to certain rules "that fall within their rights as corporations." The owners have almost unlimited power as to how they govern themselves in comparison to businesses in a more competitive environment. This leads to difficult and hard to prove questions: Are the 32-teams acting in bad faith concerning the Rooney Rule? If the owners claim that "meritocracy" is really the issue, do they have the right to pick who they want to hire? After all, the NFL is a collection of private employers. However, at the same time it must be acknowledged that in a business with 70% Black players, there is a documented absence of Black head coaches and in management.

As was to be expected the NFL quickly dismissed Flores' claims and is attempting to have the case settled through arbitration rather than going to court. The last thing the NFL wants is a legal process of discovery and testimony of witnesses that would shed light on what happens behind the scenes. Arbitration would avoid all of that and allow Roger Goodell to serve as the arbitrator. The legal team for Flores argued Goodell's role would be tainted by bias, since he was paid over $128 million dollars in salaries and bonuses by the owners during the 2020-2021 seasons. The NFL, as expected, challenged the Flores' legal team, stating:

Plaintiffs are flatly wrong that he either cannot or will not treat them fairly, and they have not remotely made the required showing. The NFL has an overriding interest in combating racism, as it has repeatedly affirmed through its statements and actions. If the Commissioner showed bias against Plaintiffs, it would undermine not only that interest but also the League's interest in upholding its system of internal dispute resolution.

THE COMMISSIONER

Paying close attention to the Flores case is the Fritz Pollard Alliance (FPA), the organization that monitors and promotes equal opportunity for coaches and executives in the NFL. Whether in the courtroom or through arbitration Flores' lawsuit seeks damages and injunctive relief in the "form of change to hiring, retention, termination, and pay transparency practices for coaching and executive positions in the NFL." Does Flores have a case? Of course, but can he win the case? That is the question.

Lost in the din of charges and countercharges is what happened to Flores when he was the coach of the Miami Dolphins. On January 10, 2022 the team fired Flores. Prior to that decision the team was purportedly seeking Sean Payton to be their new coach. The Dolphin team owner, Stephen Ross, was fined 1.5 million by the NFL for impermissible communication with Payton. The team also forfeited a 2023 first round draft pick and a 2024 third round draft pick. Ross also received a six-game suspension as a result of his actions.

All this occurred even though Flores had righted a lackluster losing team and proved his competence as an NFL head coach.

YEAR	WON	LOST	FINISH
2019	5	11	4TH IN AFC EAST
2020	10	6	2ND IN AFC EAST
2021	9	8	3RD IN AFC EAST

A last point…According to many the Giants would have gotten away with this insidious form of discrimination if New England Patriots Coach Bill Belichick had not mistakenly disclosed it to Mr. Flores in the text message. When they met with Flores that was a formality that had to be observed in order to name Brian Daboll the Head Coach. That seems to be the long and short of it.

As to Brian Flores…As his suit plays out he is now the senior defensive assistant and linebacker coach for the Pittsburgh

Steelers. Head coach Mike Tomlin hired Flores. It was fitting that Pittsburgh offered him a job. After all, this was the home of the Rooney Rule.

MIKE TOMLIN

CHAPTER 20 – LINGERING QUESTIONS AND HOPES

The January 10, 2023 copy of *USA Today* featured an article written by Tom Schad. It was entitled "Final Result: Going Beyond Numbers." The articled extensively covered comments made by Rod Graves, the Executive Director of the Fritz Pollard Alliance, the non-profit organization that seeks diversity in the NFL.

Now, as the league's coaching carousel starts to spin anew Monday, diversity advocates have mixed predictions about how coaches of color will fare during the 2023 hiring cycle. Some are pessimistic, citing the NFL owners' lackluster record of diverse hires in recent years. Others believe league initiatives and a brighter spotlight on the issue could lead to a shift.

Continuing, Graves said:

What I'm optimistic about and encouraged about is the level of attention that the owners and Roger Goodell have given this issue. Owners are particularly conscious of where this issue stands. I think they pay more attention to it. But at the end of the day, it still about results...

ROD GRAVES

Graves' words carried weight. He began his career in professional football personnel work in 1982. He was the regional scout for the Philadelphia Stars of the United States Football League. In 1984 he joined the NFL as the regional scout for the Chicago Bears. He held that position until 1993 when he was promoted to director of college scouting for the team. A year later he became director of player personnel. After 13 seasons with the Bears he joined the Arizona Cardinals. He served as the team's primary contract negotiator in addition to overseeing college and professional scouting efforts, plus dealing with salary cap management. On June 10, 2013 he joined the New York Jets as the Senior Director of Football Administration and was later the interim General Manager. On July 8, 2015 Graves left the Jets to join the NFL's front office as the Senior Vice-President of Football Administration. In time he joined the Fritz Pollard Alliance. Graves was the right man for the job. On March 28, 2022 the *Sports Business Journal* said of him:

After nearly four decades inside the NFL family, Rod Graves in 2019 stepped into a critical role outside the league with the Fritz Pollard Alliance. In his position, his primary duty is to push the league --- publically, privately and, at times, forcefully --- to embrace more diversity in hiring and promotion. Graves' brief tenure has coincided with a sea change in how the NFL talks about diversity, with Commissioner Roger Goodell pushing an expansion to the "Rooney Rule" to cover all business-side hires. But progress at the all-important head coach position has been halting at best, and Graves sits in a position of extraordinary influence as the NFL's efforts face a reckoning.

The *USA Today* article also included a comment by Mike Locksley, who founded the National Coalition of Minority Football Coaches (NCMFC) in 2020. Locksley said:

Anytime you get a minority hire, that's a win for us because there have been years where it just hasn't been there. But to put a number on what makes it successful --- to me, the success comes from the engagement and knowing that it's something that not just minority coaches want, not just the NFL executives want, but the 32 individual owners want.

Locksley credits the NFL for its recent initiatives. The NFL has expanded its Rooney Rule to require two external minority interviews for head coaching jobs, rather than one. The owners also voted to require minority interviews for quarterback coach positions, which often serves as a steppingstone to offensive coordinator and head coaching positions.

MIKE LOCKSLEY, COACH OF MARYLAND

Fritz Pollard could have written the mission statement of the NCMFC. Certainly he was an inspiring force behind the words.

Football is more than a game: it is a microcosm of life. Football, like life, presents physical and mental challenges --- true adversity in some sense --- that require innovative strategies, hard work, and perseverance. Success rarely occurs without some sacrifice, agony and pain. Even the most talented individuals cannot do it alone; rather they need the help of a team to reach the proverbial goal line.

A coach (head coach) is everything --- a teacher, a motivator, a cheerleader, a recruiter, a confidant, and on occasion, even a needed friend or parent. The relationship between coach and player is rooted in an elementary bond born of a struggle to overcome adversity in the quest of elusive success.

The NCMFC will remove the roadblocks and level the playing field for minority football coaches. Through unmatched professional training and education programs, the NCMFC will prepare its coaches for greater success. The NCMFC will highlight its member coaches' accomplishments and demonstrate their abilities using data analytics. The NCMFC will be a sounding board, a resource and an ally for all who desire meaningful diversity and inclusion in coaching by identifying minority-coaching candidates who are capable of producing on the field.

In the same *USA Today* (January 10, 2023) edition there was a thoughtful article by Mike Freeman entitled *To Panthers: Don't Overthink Wilks Decision.* The columnist made the strong argument that Steve Wilks, the interim head coach, should be hired as the fulltime coach. He pointed out that David Tepper, the owner of the team, should resist the temptation to go for a big name coach like Sean Payton or Jim Harbaugh. Instead they should select the best choice that was right in front of him and to avoid reasons not to hire a Black coach. From the writer's perspective Wilks had earned the opportunity given what he had accomplished.

STEVE WILKS

Wilks took over a sinking ship when former coach Matt Rhule was fired in October. Wilks inherited a 1-4 team that had lost 11 of its previous 12 games and had traded away its best player, running back Christian McCaffrey to San Francisco, and its second best receiver to Arizona. That was Robbie Anderson. Once he was in charge Wilks turned the team around with a 6-6 record. He stabilized the sinking ship and made the team competitive. He gained the respect of his players. Defensive lineman Derrick Brown supported Wilks, stating:

I speak for everybody in that locker room we want Wilks to be our next head coach, that's for sure. I think every week when we're going to come in, he's going to tell us how it is. He doesn't sugarcoat anything. He lets you know exactly what's going on. You could be one of the best players on the team but you walk into that building on Monday he's going to tell you exactly how you played, and that level of clarity is exactly what we want.

Though supported by his players, does that mean Wilks will get hired as the head coach? According to the writer not necessarily. Why is that? The blame rests with the owners who too often are impressed with the won-loss data. Since 2000, 15 interim coaches have taken over a team in distress. Only a very few were later made head coaches. The situation is even more pronounced for Black coaches and that was the case for Steve Wilks.

On February 7, 2023 ESPN announced that San Francisco hired Steve Wilks as their next defensive coordinator after DeMeco Ryans departed to become the head coach of the Houston Texans. 49er head coach Kyle Shanahan made it clear that he was hoping to "maintain continuity on a defense that has consistently ranked near the top of the league in recent seasons." In Wilks San Francisco is getting someone with NFL experience as a head coach, defensive coordinator, and defensive back coach.

With Wilks at the helm of the Carolina Panthers they came up just short of winning the NFC South division crown and making the playoffs. He was considered a finalist to become the Panther's head coach. The owner chose Frank Reich instead. In response to this decision Wilks posted the following on Twitter:

I'm disappointed but not defeated. Many people aren't built for this but I know what it means to persevere and see it through.

Somewhere in football heaven Fritz Pollard might have been heard saying, "I know exactly how you feel."

ESPN pointed out that Wilks landed in a spot that has been a springboard to the position of head coach. Both of Shanahan's previous defensive coordinators have gone on to be head coaches.

FRANK REICH   KYLE SHANAHAN   DEMECO RYANS

On February 17, 2023 Nancy Armour wrote a devastating critique of the NFL's hiring practices *(USA Today)*. After pointing out that the Fritz Pollard Alliance can make a list of qualified minority candidates and push for reasonable interviews under the Rooney Rule, none of it really matters. Why was that? Succinctly, the NFL owners "simply don't want a Black or brown man to be their head coach." Going on she said, "There's no way they're going to let a Black or brown man be the public face of their franchise, front and center on TV screens for the better part of three hours every Sunday." Pressing on she noted that in the current NFL hiring cycle the results were "shameful as always." Five head coaches were hired. Only one was Black. That brought the grand total of Black head coaches to three in a 32-team league where, if it must be stated, at least 60% of the players are Black. This has been the case since Art Shell became the first Black coach in the modern NFL era and that was thirty years ago. It was also twenty years ago that the Rooney Rule was adopted.

To bolster her case (or indictment) Armour focused on the case of Eric Bieniemy, the offensive coach of the Kansas City Chiefs. He tutored Patrick Mahomes into a Super Bowl start. He helped the Chiefs win two Super Bowls in the last four years. The team's offense is constantly among the best. It was number 1 twice in the last five years. According to the head coach of Kansas City, Andy Reid, "Eric Bieniemy was tremendous down the stretch there, putting things together." What was Reid referring to? Those who saw the game know. It was the second half turnaround in the Super Bowl against the Philadelphia Eagles. The Chiefs scored on every possession to erase a 10-point deficit and win the game, 38 to 35. One would think any team in need of an elite head coach would consider Bieniemy, but that was not the case. Only one of five teams with openings interviewed him and he didn't make the Indianapolis Colts' list of finalists. For Armour's take Bieniemy's case is at the heart of the matter. "The owners are the only ones who can level the playing field for Black and brown coaches, and that's just not going to happen in their backyards." To be fair Armour did quote the NFL Commissioner Roger Goodell about the NFL and diversity.

We always look to sort of say, "How can we do better?" A number of things we implemented last year have proven to be a direct beneficiary of some of the changes that occurred.

What Goodell really meant by this nuanced statement Armour was unable to decipher.

ANDY REID AND ERIC BIENIEMY

It is fair to ask if Eric Bieniemy will ever be a head coach. The answer may not rest completely with the owners, the Rooney Rule, or the constant pressure of the Pollard Alliance. Andy Reid is now 65 and has nothing left to prove. He will walk into the Pro Football Hall of Fame. Perhaps as a parting gift to his offensive coordinator and in fairness to all Black football players he'll anoint Bieniemy his successor and hope that management follows suit. One can hope. If not this perhaps Bieniemy will move on to another team, again seeking the elusive head coaching position he richly deserves.

In this mix of lingering questions and eternal hopes a great drama is being played out on the football field, the baseball diamond, and the basketball court, and in every other aspect of our social life. Is it possible to eliminate systemic racism? This was at the core of Colin Kaepernick's message when he said, "Injustice toward one group of Americans hurts us all." And wasn't that Fritz Pollard's quest, which he sought with quiet grace and indefatigable dignity.

FREDERICK DOUGLAS "FRITZ" POLLARD (1/27/1894 – 5/11/1980)

LEGACIES

FREDERICK DOUGLASS "FRITZ" POLLARD

Perhaps you will visit Washington D.C. some day. When you do cross into Maryland and find your way to Fort Lincoln Cemetery. With a little help from one of the attendants find your way to the gravesite of Frederick Douglass "Fritz" Pollard. Once there take a few minutes to reflect on his life and a few words this gifted athlete once shared with the world:

Football isn't a game. It is religion. The ball is your life.

If you drop it, that's a different story.

Fritz didn't drop the ball between the goal posts. His induction into the College Football Hall of Fame in 1954 and the Pro Football Hall of Fame in 2005 attests to his remarkable feats on the gridiron that included two seasons at the collegiate level and seven years in professional football. All that will be remembered as you gaze at his gravesite. But there will also be other memories besides his football heroics at Brown University or with the Akron Indians where he was a dazzling halfback and assistant coach. You will also reflect on what he endured as a Black man playing in a white man's game. He experienced racial insults, threats on his life, and physical abuse from opposing teams. Unfortunately, for too many white fans and players he was a villain cloaked in football attire and cleats. He was a Black man challenging white supremacy at a time when intolerance reigned. Somehow, he survived and in time many fans came to appreciate him as a fine player, but also as a businessman later in life and a civil rights activist. To many Black Americans, he was a hero who demanded respect, certainly for himself and also for his race. As you depart pause for one last lingering moment to again see this diminutive player darting downfield in the Yale Bowl, fleet-footed and daring as he left Yale players in his wake. See him again in the 1915 Rose Bowl mired in the mud of a drenching storm, the first Black man to play in the "granddaddy of all bowl games." And always remember him for clinging tightly to the ball through-out his life, refusing to permit prejudice and bigotry to diminish him as a man.

PAUL EUGENE BROWN

Coach Brown played a major role in bringing the first Black players into the American Football Conference (AFC) immediately after World War II. In doing so he ended the ban on Black players in professional football, though not in the National Football Conference. Brown's decision was, of course, the fulfillment of Fritz Pollard's dream for an integrated professional league.

About this effort, Jim Brown, the great running back for the Cleveland Browns, said:

He integrated pro football without uttering a single word about integration. He just went out, signed a bunch of great Black athletes, and started kicking butt. That's how you do it. You don't talk about it. He never said one word about race. This was a time when in sports when you'd play in some cities and the white players could stay at the nice hotel, but the blacks had to stay in the homes of some Black families in town. But not with Paul. We always stayed in hotels that took the entire team. Again, he never said a word. But in his own way, the man integrated football the right way --- and no one was going to stop him.

Brown was inducted into the Pro Football Hall of Fame in 1967.

COACH BROWN

JOHN WESLEY CARLOS

On October 10, 2011 John Carlos recalled his raised "fist" in Mexico City when he again raised his fist at an Occupy Wall Street demonstration. In recalling what he did on the Olympic podium on October 16, 1968 he said:

Today I am here for you. Why? Because I am you...We're here forty-three years later because there's a fight still to be won. This day is not for us but for our children to come."

Carlos was also quoted as saying:

In life, there's the beginning and the end. The beginning doesn't matter. The end doesn't matter. All that matters is what you do in between --- whether you're prepared to do what it takes to make change.

Putting Carlos' actions in perspective...

With his actions he joined the ranks of Mohammad Ali, Curt Flood, and Jackie Robinson and a host of other activist athletes. These men used their celebrity and status to bring international attention to America's pervasive racism and white supremacy placing their hard-won privileges at risk to make visible the unacceptable conditions of less privileged Black people in America.

In 2005, a statue depicting Carlos and Tommie Smith on the medal stand was dedicated on the campus of San Jose State University. On July 16, 2008, Carlos and Smith accepted the Arthur Ashe Award for Courage for their salute at the ESPY Awards in Los Angeles, California.

ERNIE DAVIS

Davis was the All-American football player from Syracuse University and the first Black winner of the Heisman Memorial Trophy in 1961. He was drafted by the Washington Redskins to end the team's ban against Black players. Refusing to play for the team with a racist tradition he was traded to the Cleveland Browns. He never played a single down for the team. He was stricken with leukemia and died on May 19, 1963 at Cleveland Lakeside Hospital. He was only 23 years old. He was elected to the College Football Hall of Fame in 1979. Each year the state of New York hosts the best high school players in the Ernie Davis Classic on Thanksgiving Day. A statue of Davis is on the Syracuse University campus where pre-game pep rallies are held. Davis is buried at Woodlawn Cemetery in Elmira, New York.

In his own words he said of his life:

But when I look back I can't call myself unlucky. My 23rd birthday was December 12. In these years I have had more than most people get in a lifetime.

He later said:

Someplace along the line you have to come to an understanding with yourself, and I had reached mine a long time before, when I was still in the hospital. Either you fight or you give up.

Ernie Davis never played a game as a professional with his only appearance at Cleveland Stadium coming during a 1962 pre-season game, in which he ran onto the field as a spotlight followed him. Following his death, the Browns retired his number 45 jersey.

DAVIS AND THE HEISMAN

MEMORIAL ON THE SYRACUSE CAMPUS

WILLIAM HENRY "LONE STAR" DIETZ

Coach Dietz, the former coach of the 1916 Washington State football team, died from cancer on July 20, 1964 at the St. Joseph Hospital in Reading, Pennsylvania one month before his 80th birthday. He was inducted into the College Hall of Fame as a coach in 2012. He was also inducted into the Indian Hall of Fame in 1983, as well as the Pennsylvania Sports Hall of Fame in 1997.

THE COACH AND HIS COUGAR TEAM – 1915

Years later Dietz recalled his 1916 Washington State Rose Bowl team that tackled Fritz Pollard and upset Brown University. He said of his team:

There has never been a team with a finer spirit --- we were all for each other. We emphasized how much depended on every man doing his job in his position, each helping the others, and that was the spirit in which we went through the season and played in the Rose Bowl.

At the time of his death he had a copy of a quotation from a book he had helped Pop Warner write. It seemed to reflect his whole life:

*When the game is pretty tough
Don't you ever holler "nuff"
Show the world you have the
stuff Keep a-goin.*

COUGARS TEAM TOURING PASADENA - 1916

WILLIAM CLAIRE HALLEY HARDING

When the Cleveland Rams came to Los Angeles Harding was the sports writer who pushed to end the ban against Black football players in the NFL. He died on April 1, 1967 in Chicago, Illinois. He was 67 years old. Those who knew him respected his commitment to social change.

He never backed down. He never crumbled. He'd go up every day and fought the good fight for Black athletic advancement in pro sports, his family, and our community no matter what, even when it sometimes seemed like he was fighting alone. He taught us to stand strong and be accountable for our beliefs and inalienable rights despite all odds.

Seen with perspective…By forcing the NFL to sign Black players the color ban was finally erased. This was one more thing Black reporters did in advocating for societal changes in America. The eventual integration of the military services was another thing that Black reporters had a huge role in pushing for over the years. As Black reporters they envisioned Fritz Pollard's hope for the integration of professional sports.

According to Harding's family he harbored some regrets concerning his own athletic career.

He knew how good he could have been. He knew he could have made it in the big time with a fair shot, but he did not have that opportunity. That sadness and weariness never left him during his life.

LOST CHAMPIONS
Four Men, Two Teams, and the Breaking of Pro Football's Color Line

#10

Black Sportswriters in Los Angeles

In the 1940s L.A. boasted three major black weeklies and though black sportswriters pushed hardest for integration their efforts have mostly been whitewashed. (Incl. above: Halley Harding, LA Tribune; Eddie Burbridge, California Eagle; Abie Robinson, LA Sentinel)

AS A YOUNG PLAYER   HARDING, RIGHT SIDE, THIRD FROM FRONT

Harding was buried in Burr Oak Cemetery in Alsip, Illinois. There are more than a dozen Negro Leagues players buried there, too, and if one looks carefully the graves of Emmett Till and heavy-weight boxing champion Ezzard Charles are also there, finally all reclining in peace.

CHARLES FREDERICK HOLDER

The tradition of a Rose Bowl football game began with a scholar and sportsman in 1902. He recommended a college game bringing together two outstanding teams. This he accomplished.

First Tournament East-West Football Game
Jan. 1, 1902 - Michigan vs Stanford

Holder died in Pasadena, California as a result of an automo-bile accident. He was 64 years old. He was buried in Mountain View Cemetery in Altadena, California. A memorial plaque at the north end of Avalon Harbor, Santa Catalina Island reads:

This tablet is placed here by friends of the naturalist who devoted himself to the preservation of wild game and sea life; who awakened the public conscience to the rights of birds and beast and fish, and whose work won at once the approval of sportsmen and the tribute of nations.

JACK ARTHUR JOHNSON

On July 4, 1910 Jackson, the first Black heavyweight cham-pion, fought James J. Jeffries in a 15 round brawl that ended with the former champion and the so-called "White Man's Hope", unable to continue. A TKO. Almost immediately Johnson's victory led to widespread race riots across the United States.

Johnson died on June 10, 1946 in Raleigh, North Carolina following a car accident in Franklinton, North Carolina. He was 68 years old. He was buried at Graceland Cemetery in Chicago. John-son was inducted into *Ring Magazine's* Boxing Hall of Fame in 1954. He was inducted into the International Boxing Hall of Fame in 1993. In 2005 the United States National Film Preservation Board "deemed the film of the 1910 Johnson-Jefferies fight historically significant" and put it in the National Film Registry. In 2012 the City of Galveston, Texas dedicated a park in Johnson's memory as Galveston Island's most famous native son. The park is called the Jack Johnson Park. The Park includes a life-size bronze statue of the prizefighter. In his own way Johnson was a Fritz Pollard with box-ing gloves, stating "I want to be treated with respect."

JOHNSON-JEFFRIES FIGHT OF THE CENTURY AND RACE RIOTS

JAMES WELDON JOHNSON

He is remembered for writing the lyrics for "Lift Every Voice and Sing." That music later became known as the Negro National Anthem. He died in 1938 in Wiscasset, Maine. He was 67 years old. Over 2,000 people attended his funeral in Harlem. His ashes were interred at Green-Wood Cemetery in Brooklyn, New York. In 1925 the NAACP awarded him the Spingarn Medal for outstanding achievement by an American Negro. In 1933 he was given the W.E.B. DuBois Prize for literature. In 2007 Emory University in Atlanta created the James Weldon Johnson Institute for the Study of Race and Difference. On February 2, 1988 the United States Post Office issued a 22-cent stamp in his honor. Fritz Pollard would have been proud.

It was said of Johnson:

Johnson's rise to champion signified Black possibilities at a mo-ment in time when all of the regular channels of Black success, whether it be trying to get a quality education or trying to make it in business or even just trying to be involved in politics --- because there was so much widespread disenfranchisement --- this was an example of a success that couldn't be disputed.

RAYMOND HOWARD KEMP

Kemp was a charter member of the Pittsburgh Pirates football team (now called the Steelers). He was also the first Black player in the team's history. In 1933 he was the only Black on the team and by 1933 only one of two Blacks still in the NFL before the ban kept the game all white until 1946. In 1982 the Steelers celebrated their 50th anniversary. Kemp was remembered and invited to Three Rivers Stadium to participate in the ceremonies. He was the last surviving member of the 1933 team. Kemp died on March 26, 2002 in Ashtabula, Ohio. He was 94 years old. About his life he said: *I decided that I was going to the coalmines (with his dad) and I was going to come out to be the baddest football player in the country.*

Kemp's time with the Pirates was bittersweet. Once when the team was in NYC for a game with the Giants. Kemp later remembered:

They assigned the Pirate players to their rooms and I was left standing there. The traveling secretary for the team said: "Ray, I want to introduce you to the assistant manager of the hotel." We were in New York and my guard was completely down. This man said, "Ray it seems we have a problem. We are sorry; we just don't have any room. We were wondering if you could stay at the YMCA, the Harlem branch of the YMCA." Well I had no alternative but to say, "Yes, I can imagine I can." That was one of the longest walks in my life --- to walk from the desk to the front door of the hotel.

At the end of the season he was cut from the team. No other Black football player would be in the NFL until Kenny Washington in 1946.

Kemp was eventually recognized by the Pro Football Hall of Fame as one of the Black pioneers in the game. Duquesne University honored him in their Sports Hall of Fame. He was also inducted into the Western Pennsylvania Sports Hall of Fame. He received an Outstanding Educator Award from the Conference of the Pennsylvania Black Basic Education Association.

KEMP, BACK ROW, 4TH FROM THE RIGHT

WILLIAM H. LEWIS

He was the first Black football player to be selected as an All-American, while playing at Harvard. He was also one of the first Blacks to be admitted to the American Bar Association in 1911. During his long life he was elected and appointed to many public offices, including Assistant Attorney-General under President William Taft. This was the highest federal position to which any Black had ever been appointed. The appointment was bitterly fought by southern members of the Senate. According to one Georgia newspaper:

Many southern members are firmly resolved that Lewis shall never be elevated to the high post of one of the five assistant attorneys general. The position carries with it a handsome salary, high social position and an entrée to White House functions. Whether or not Lewis would ever avail himself other privileges, a number of southern Democrats feel that they do not want to be party to elevating him to an eminence where such recognition would be his as a matter of official right.

In 1912, Lewis built a successful private practice. He earned a reputation as an outstanding trial lawyer and became one of the first Black attorneys to join the legal team of the newly created National Association for the Advancement of Colored People (NAACP).

JOE LILLARD

Along with Ray Kemp he was the last Black football player in the NFL in 1932 as a running back for the Chicago Cardinals. He was nick-named "The Midnight Express" by the media. In 1933 he scored almost half of all Cardinal points. It wasn't enough. The ban's net entangled him. In his few NFL games he was known as a fighter that wouldn't back down to vicious racial taunts and excessively brutal hits by the opposition. As one writer said:

A rival player would provoke Lillard, and Lillard would fight back. At a time when Black athletes were expected to perform the act of stoicism known as "taking it," Lillard's retaliations were regarded by all whites and many Blacks as prideful foolishness, if not sheer lunacy.

In his own way Lillard struggled against the racism afflicting pro-fessional sports in his day. He established his own professional basketball team, the Chicago Hottentotts. He also tried to form a Negro League composed of banned players of color (1936-1937). He was unsuccessful in these endcavors but, as did Fritz Pollard, he fought against a stacked deck. It is a little known fact that Lillard played for Fritz Pollard's Brown Bombers. Such is the fickleness of history. In 1933 the Chicago Cardinals played the Pittsburgh Pirates, Joe Lillard against Ray Kemp --- the last two Blacks in the NFL until 1946.

Joe Lillard of the Chicago Cardinals, number 19, being chased by Red Grange, number 77, in a 1933 NFL game.
(Courtesy of the Saint Louis Cardinals)

MARION MOTLEY

Motley was one of the first two blacks to play professional foot-ball following WWII. Along with Bill Willis he was offered a contract by Paul Brown to play for the Cleveland Browns in the American Football League. The date was August 10, 1946. Motley signed for $4,000. He ended his playing days with an average of 5.7 yards per carry, a record that remains unbroken. In his career he gained 4,720 yards and scored 31 touchdowns, while blocking with ferocity and also playing linebacker. It was said of him that he had "no equal as a blocker. He could run with any-body for 30 yards and he was a great, great linebacker." In 1968 Motley was voted into the Pro Football Hall of Fame. He was the second Black to receive this honor. The first was Emlen Tunnell of the New York Giants.

Paul Brown said of his player.

He was a powerhouse on both sides of the ball, as a fullback and linebacker. Offensively, he was used in four different basic plays, the draw, the trap, the sweep, and the screen pass. Opponents knew what was coming and still couldn't stop him.

Late in life he said of his football days…"I was fortunate to be able to be one of the few to excel at something I liked to do." In 1994 he was named to the NFL's 75th Anniversary All-Time Team. In 2019 he was selected as one of the twelve running backs on the NFL 100 All-Time Team. He died on June 27, 1999 in Cleveland, Ohio. He was 79 years old.

MOTLEY　　　　　　　　　　　TUNNELL

PETER NORMAN

Norman was the man in the middle in Mexico City when two Black Americans raised their fists in opposition to racial violence in the United States during the playing of the Star Spangled Banner. The Australian Olympic Committee criticized his support of Tom-mie Smith and Juan Carolos. He was boycotted from the 1972 Aus-tralian Olympic team. Years later a statue of Norman on the 1968 medal podium with Smith and Carlos was unveiled at the National Museum of African American History and Culture in Washington D.C. On October 11, 2012 the Australian House of Representatives passed an apology motion, stating:

We acknowledge the bravery of Peter Norman in donning an Olympic Project for Human Rights badge on the podium in solidar-ity with African-American athletes Tommie Smith and John Carlos, who gave the "Black Power" salute.

We apologize to Peter Norman for the treatment he received upon his return to Australia, and the failure to fully recognize his inspirational role.

Norman died of a heart attack on October 3, 2006 in Mel-bourne. He was 64 years old. The United States Track and Field Federation proclaimed October 9, 2006, the day of his funeral, as Peter Norman Day. Tommie Smith and John Carlos gave eulogies at his funeral.

John Carlos said of him…

Peter was a lone soldier. He consciously chose to be a sacrificial lamb in the name of human rights. There's no one more than him that Australia should honor, recognize, and appreciate.

Tommie Smith said of him…

He paid the price with his choice. It wasn't just a simple gesture to help us; it was HIS fight. He was a white man, a white Australian man standing with two men of color, standing up in the moment of victory, all in the name of the same thing.

HE CAME IN SECOND BUT WAS A TRUE CHAMPION

ROBERT "BOBBY" WELLS MARSHALL

Marshall was the first Black to play football in the Western Conference, today known as the Big Ten. Along with Fritz Pollard he was one of the first two Blacks to play in the NFL. Upon retiring from his government job in 1950 in Minnesota, he was honored with a testimonial dinner for his service to the public and his exploits on the gridiron and in other fields. He was the first Black to graduate from Minnesota's law school. He was the first Black appointed to the state grain department. He worked there for 39 years. He was also the first Black to play professional hockey when he signed with an independent team in Pennsylvania. It was said of Marshall:

He was an outstanding man of the Minneapolis African American community. His greatest contributions may not have been on the field of play. He stood as a reminder to all Minnesotans that African Americans had integrity and ability on and off the playing field during the decades when they were banned from professional sports and many other opportunities.

Marshall died of Alzheimer's disease in 1958. He was 73 years old. He was inducted into the College Football Hall of Fame in 1971.

DAN REEVES

Reeves was instrumental in bringing professional football to Los Angeles, thereby beginning the expansion of the NFL across the nation. He is credited as the first NFL owner to sign a Black player in 1946. That was Kenny Washington. In doing so he ended the ban against Black players.

It is a little known fact that Reeves gave his approval to a Ram player --- Fred Gehrke --- to paint Ram horns on his helmet. Today all teams display team symbols on helmets. In 1967 Reeves was enshrined in the Pro Football Hall of Fame. He was honored by the Los Angeles Memorial Coliseum with a "Court of Honor" plaque. He died on April 15, 1971 of Hodgkin's disease in New York City.

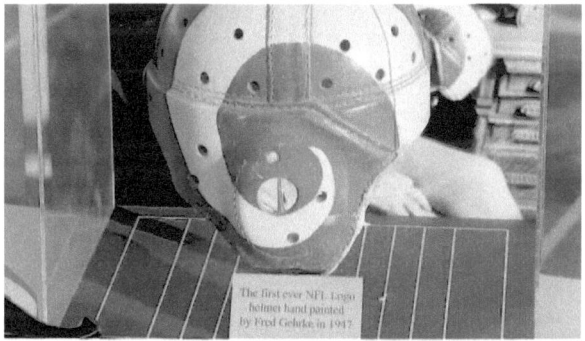

The first ever NFL Logo helmet hand painted by Fred Gehrke in 1947

EDWARD NORTH "ROBBIE" ROBINSON

The former Brown University coach of Fritz Pollard died on March 10, 1945 at Corey Hill Hospital in Brookline, Massachusetts. He was 73 years old. He was inducted into the College Hall of Fame in 1955. He was one of four Brown alumni to receive such an honor. The others were John Heisman, Wallace Wade, and Fritz Pollard. He was known as the "father of Brown football" after compiling a 157-4-1 record. His 1916 Rose Bowl team was integrated.

1892 – ROBINSON TOP ROW, CENTER

COACH ROBINSON BRINGS AN INTEGRATED
TEAM TO THE 1916 ROSE BOWL

AUGUSTA SAVAGE

The sculptor of "The Harp" for the 1939 New York World Fair died on March 27, 1962. She was 50 years old. A public high school in Baltimore, Maryland was named after her --- the Augusta Fells Savage Institute of Visual Arts. Her home and studio in Sau-gerties, New York was listed on the New York and National Register of Historic Places. The city of Green Cove Springs, Florida nom-inated her to the Florida Artist Hall of Fame. She was inducted in 2008. Her legacy was in her work.

AT WORK ON THE HARP

ART SHELL

Shell was the second Black NFL head coach and the first hired in the modern era when the Los Angeles Raiders owner, Al Davis, offered him a contract in 1989. Recall the first Black head coach was Fritz Pollard. Shell was named the AFC Coach of the Year in 1990. He was named to the Pro Football Hall of Fame in 1989. In 1999 he was ranked number 55 on *The Sporting News'* list of the 100 greatest Football Players. In 2013 he was inducted into the College Hall of Fame.

About becoming the head coach of the Raiders, Shell said:

It was a historic event and I understood the significance of it. But the main thing was, I know who I am and I'm proud of it...But I'm also a Raider and I don't believe the color of my skin entered into this decision...If you know Al Davis and you know this organi-zation, you'll understand that.

Referring to Al Davis he said:

I could not have gotten to where I got without (Davis) be-cause he gave me an opportunity to be a player; he gave me an opportunity to be an assistant coach, head football coach, and to coach that football team twice...

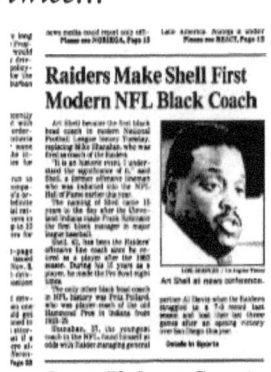

Raiders Make Shell First Modern NFL Black Coach

OZZIE SIMMONS

He is remembered as an exceptional running back for the University of Iowa and as a Black player banned from the NFL in the 1930's. He was nicknamed the "Ebony Ell" and was one of the first Black All-Americans in the 1930's. He was also subject to abuse from both fans and the opposing teams. He was a target on the football field causing him to sustain numerous injuries. In the 1935 game against the Minnesota Gophers the physical attacks were bla-tant. At the time discrimination was a way of life on the Minnesota campus. Dormitories were segregated. The nursing program was a white-only deal. School dances were essentially for whites only. No University employee was Black. This odious treatment permeated the Gopher football team and was the underlying cause of the vi-cious attacks on Simmons.

As Simmons said:

They piled on me and kneed me. The refs didn't stop it. No penalties were called.

How did Simmons handle all this? I heard the words…

Let's get that n---r over there. Come on n---r, you're not go-ing to run today. I didn't say anything, because I learned the best way to do it was just play your game and don't say anything.

Simmons lettered from 1934-1936. Unable to crack the NFL ban on Black players he played professional football for the Patter-son Panthers of the American association, 1937-1939. He was a first team all-league player in 1939. Later in life he spent four decades teaching physical education in the Chicago schools.

Simmons was inducted into the Bob Douglas Black Sports Hall of Fame in New York in 1964. In 1989 he was selected as an all-time running back for Iowa University's 100th anniversary of col-legiate football. He died in 2001 from complications from Alzheimer's and Parkinson's disease. He was 87 years old. He was buried in a black sport coat. Stitched in gold on the coat were the words "Hall of Fame."

TOMMIE SMITH

1968 was a turbulent time in America --- an unending tragedy in Southeast Asia, rioting in the streets, a country unhinged by violence in Vietnam and in Chicago. Into this maelstrom of pain and suffering came a raised fist in the Olympics. The magazines of the day captured the fury of the moment.

Smith said of the Mexico City protest:

We were not Antichrists. We were just human beings who saw a need to bring attention to the inequality in our country. There was nothing but a raised fist in the air and a bowed head, acknowledging the American flag --- not symbolizing a hatred for it.

In 1978 he became a member of the United States National Track and Field Hall of Fame. In 1996 he was inducted into the California Black Sports Hall of Fame. In 2013 Goddard College honored Smith as an alumnus by awarding him the Presidential Award for Activism.

WOODROW WILSON WOOLWINE STRODE

Strode died of lung cancer on December 31, 1994 in Glendora, California. He was 80 years old. He was buried at Riverside National Cemetery in Riverside, California. Due to the many western films he appeared in over the years he was inducted into the Black Filmmakers Hall of Fame in 1980. In 2021 he was inducted into the Hall of Great Westerners of the National Cowboy and Western Heritage Museum.

Strode had attended UCLA where he paired with Jackie Robinson and Kenny Washington in the backfield. What a lineup! After graduation and a stint in the service, he joined Washington by signing a contract with the Los Angeles Rams to end the NFL ban on Black players. Later he said of his decision and the adversity it brought him…

"If I have to integrate heaven, I don't want to go."

Following his short Ram days he began a lifetime career in Hollywood, and in the process paved the way for future Black film actors. His commanding presence made him a desired actor in such films as *The Ten Commandments, Spartacus,* and *Sergeant Rutledge.*

In Pork Chop Hill the world of movie fiction and the city streets of Los Angeles merged. In a scene in which Strode played a reluctant soldier in the Korean War a superior officer reminds him that all the guys are fighting. Why not you? His answer still resonates today:

But you ought to see where I live back home. You SOB I wouldn't die for that and I'll be goddam if I'm going to fight for Korea.

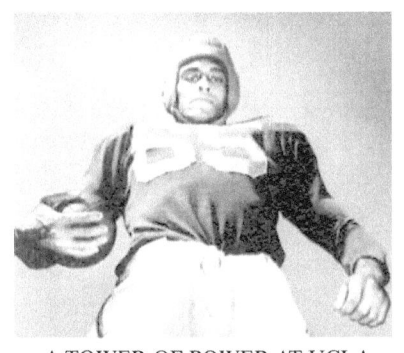

WOODY STRODE **End**

A TOWER OF POWER AT UCLA

WILLIAM WALLACE WADE

The former teammate of Fritz Pollard at Brown University and with the Akron professional football team died on October 6, 1986 in Durham, North Carolina. He was 94 years old. He was bur-ied in Maplewood Cemetery in Durham. He was inducted into the College Hall of Fame in 1955. In 1967, Duke University renamed its football stadium Wallace Wade Stadium in his honor. In 2006, a bronze statue of Wade was erected outside of the University of Alabama Bryant-Denny Stadium. There he joined four other head coaches who had led Alabama to national championships: Frank Thomas, Bear Bryant, Gene Stallings, and Nick Saban.

COACH WADE, THE MAN WHO SUPPORTED POLLARD

KENNETH STANLEY WASHINGTON

Washington died of heart and lung problems in Los Ange-les, California in 1971. He was 52 years old. He is buried in the Evergreen Cemetery in Los Angeles. He was honored with a Los Angeles Memorial Coliseum "Court of Honor" plaque. He was in-ducted to the College Football Hall of Fame in 1956. UCLA retired his number 13-jersey in the same year. He was also inducted into the UCLA Athletic Hall of Fame. His alma mater Abraham Lincoln High School awards the Kenny Washington Trophy to the school's best football player each year.

Washington will always be remembered as the man who broke the NFL ban on Black football players in 1946.

Kenny Washington Signs With L. A. Rams

KENNY WASHINGTON

LOS ANGELES — (NNPA) — Kenny Washington, former All-American halfback at UCLA, last Thursday signed a contract with the Los Angeles Rams of the National Football League.

The championship Rams, recently transplanted from Cleveland, purchased the 27-year-old star's contract from the Hollywood Bears of the Pacific Coast League for an unspecified sum.

Washington, in signing the pact, became the first colored athlete to perform in the National loop since Joe Lillard of Oregon played with the Chicago Cardinals in 1933.

Charles F. (Chile) Walsh, general manager of the Rams refused College All-Stars at Soldier's Field, Chicago.

* * *

THE FIRST member of his race contracted by a National League club in 13 years, Washington assumes a position in football similar to that of his former teammate at UCLA, Jackie Robinson, Negro infielder signed by the Brooklyn Dodgers for their Montreal farm.

In its infancy, the National League had such Negro standouts as Fritz Pollard at Akron, Ink Williams, Bob Marshall, Sol Butler and Duke Slater at Rock Island. Slater, one of the all-time tackle Titans, later starred for the Chicago Cardinals.